W9-BLN-970

MESSAGES FROM MY
HANDS

Dick -
The unique conditions of
our connection have fostered a
genuine honest friendship.
I value our relationship and
trust it will endure.

Love Beth
Mary Beth

MESSAGES FROM MY
HANDS

MARY BETH EGELING

Copyright © 2008 by Mary Beth Egeling.

Library of Congress Control Number:		2008905048
ISBN:	Hardcover	978-1-4363-4480-7
	Softcover	978-1-4363-4479-1

All rights reserved. No part of this book may be reproduced or transmitted in any form or by any means, electronic or mechanical, including photocopying, recording, or by any information storage and retrieval system, without permission in writing from the copyright owner.

This book was printed in the United States of America.

To order additional copies of this book, contact:
Xlibris Corporation
1-888-795-4274
www.Xlibris.com
Orders@Xlibris.com
43177

Contents

For Shannon and Heather
Both call me home

Preface

Recently, I had an important discussion with the Reverend Michael Capron. I am his dental hygienist from days long past, before he was a reverend and before I became a massage therapist. *Way* before my deliverance. I left the office at which he is a patient to pursue my education. A time after I completed school and began building my massage practice, I was looking for work to supplement my income. I took a part-time position at the same office I left and was pleased to discover that Michael remained a patient; I always liked him. We reconnected in the very treatment room where we first met.

During his cleaning appointment, we took some time to refamiliarize each other with our lives since we had last parted over ten years prior. Conversation came to this then-completed-but-not-yet-submitted manuscript. I told him that the book was about my reintroduction to the power, energy, and wisdom of the Universe, how my timely liberation came about because of it.

After hearing my description, he told me that he had a little trouble with my nomenclature; he had difficulty wrapping his head around the concept. That giving the name "the Universe" to what he knew to be God seemed a bit too impersonal for him. I assured him that we were in fact both speaking of the same thing: that *my* name for the omnipotent force that creates all, nourishes all, and guides all holds the same significance and sacredness as *his* name for what we were both speaking of.

He nodded. I smiled. We continued our comfortable conversation.

Chapter One

MARIAN

Marian's skin is black. Not dark. Not brown. Not even "ebony" could describe it. Black like pitch. Black like a starless night in the woods. Black like india ink black.

My skin is white. Not fair. Not light. Describing it as pale is completely inadequate. White like a marshmallow. White like Elmer's school glue. White like geisha-makeup white.

Our two skins together made a striking contrast. This observation may seem overly obvious. Of course, we made quite a contrast. But it was through this dissimilarity that, for me, clarity came.

I met Marian long before I got my license to practice massage therapy. We met in the dental chair, so to speak. I was working as a dental hygienist in a prophy mill office while pursuing my education. I liked her instantly, and the relationship was immediately comfortable. Every three to four months, she would come to the office to get her teeth cleaned. Over time, talk turned, as it usually does, to more personal aspects of each other's lives. The mere mention of my current educational endeavor caused her to jump in the chair. She had always wanted a massage—couldn't afford one, being a lower-rung social service employee in a sinking support office.

As she spoke of her desires, I had a private side conversation with myself. Massage instructors at school had informed us that we were welcome to practice techniques on persons, but we were forbidden to charge them as we had no license to practice therapy and doing so would constitute breaking the law. As Marian finished speaking, she gazed wantonly past the dental light throwing a rectangle of light on her mouth. I stated that I needed people to practice on and asked her if she would be willing to be my guinea pig. She shrieked that she would love it, but then, looking cautiously sidewayslike, inquired how much it was going to set her back. I told her with a smile that it was free—I couldn't charge until I got my license, wouldn't be legal. She accepted with praise be to God, and stated that *sometimes* when you really need it, your prayers are answered. So it was. Later that day, we spoke on the phone and scheduled an hour for me to practice on her.

In typical fashion, I have patients start facedown; when I enter the room, their back is covered by linens. In order to begin, I undraped her form. Marian had a great expanse of back. From the moment I began the massage, all I could see were my small white hands on the vast sable background.

I've touched dark skin many times: Certainly in my many years as a dental hygienist. Playing dolls with my little girlfriend in kindergarten. Making out in the woods with Amory at a party, toward the end of high school. My more intimate, mature relationship with Mr. Jones a number of years back. Abundant meetings and handshakes and hugs with so many people darker complexioned than me. The experiences never elicited a particular insight into how I saw myself relative to the rest of the universe.

I look at my hands all the time when I work. I am undeniably familiar with my enlarged knuckles and the bend and degree of turn of each finger. The permanent indent where Michael's ring rests when I am not working. The scar from the time I sliced my thumb open on a can of beans. The remnant of a stubborn wart I tried so hard to hide while in grade school. The path that each vein takes to return blood to my heart. Seeing my hands this time was quite different.

The gloss on her skin from the massage gel heightened the contrast of the matte finish of my hands. I became enthralled by their movement and undulation. Heavy, gross movements. Light, delicate maneuvers. After a while, it seemed to me as if I was watching motion I had no part in controlling, like observing a master demonstrate massage techniques. I became aware, in the strangest detached-yet-connected way, of the texture and temperature gradients as I worked the muscles of her body.

Marian didn't speak much—in fact, not at all. The stillness and the hushed music and the flood of sensory input provided an opportunity for unique thoughts and images to flow into me. While I was working on her leg, I imagined a great dark pillar of a pier, embedded in the cold sand beneath the churning waters of the North Atlantic. A thick unmoving support to the boardwalk above. My hands were the water rhythmically pulsing up and around and against and about, pushing then pulling back just to start the endless cycle over and over again. Whitecaps forming and moving across the deep dark waters.

My hands became an ancient glacier, comprised of uncountable tiny frozen droplets of water yet collectively an unstoppable force, slowly grinding along the base of a great sparse dark mountain. Carving a valley in which future life would take hold.

I saw that my hands, like water, have an erosive quality. That through repetition and perseverance girded with calm pressure, they could change, over time, any surface they worked against.

I observed the deftness and the wisdom with which they proceeded. The confidence and intuition they demonstrated. The heat they generated and the scents they released with their warmth. Their fearless foray to places my mind routinely proved inadequate and unprepared to go. All this without thinking about it. It had little to do with me. I became aware I was simply a conduit, a vehicle through which the energy of the Universe entered and flowed back and forth.

It then stunned me to recognize I have always read and navigated the world through my outer covering. Anything I have ever really learned or observed has been through my hands or my skin. It is as though they have been the singular valid entry route to my head. The only paper the truth could be written on. What I heard or observed didn't mean anything until I felt it.

I can remember collecting stones and sea glass at the beach as a child. I would hold them in my hands and turn them over and over again in my fingers. I could feel their formation, their history. Their soul. Like me, they had been tumbled and battered and tossed about for far too long. But they were more beautiful because of it. They were definitely worth saving.

As a girl, I sat on our front stoop, conversing with the wind. As it blew across my face and chest, I recognized that my body was a small stop on its great journey around and about the globe; and that in blowing past, it took a small piece of me to somewhere else. Fragments of other places entered and exited my lungs as I breathed out my tiny contribution to this collective force, one of the many that connect us all.

I just *had* to touch everything. I was very much about texture and tactility. Resistance and glide. Degrees of firmness and temperature. My mother would go mad every time I walked by the butcher block and put my hand on whatever just came out of the oven. I didn't just touch it—I had to press on it too. I loved to feel the warmth and consistency. I handled my food before I ate and reveled in those things permissible to eat without utensils, like fried chicken or pizza or cupcakes. To this day, when I make cookies for my patients, I lovingly shape the dough with my fingers before putting the moist, cool uncooked morsels on the cookie sheets.

I gingerly handled broken bits of glass when I came across them, tested the spike of barbed wire, deftly passed my index finger through a candle flame. Became familiar with the smooth sticky slipperiness of blood. Do Not Touch signs were a special invitation for me; I had to disregard the instruction. The information and understanding I would derive from contact with such forbidden things was worth the slight risk of damage or personal injury.

Whenever possible, I would immerse my entire body in the experience. I would bury myself in the sand. Sit in the mud. Roll in the snow. Run out in the rain. Lie faceup on the asphalt to see what the sun had to offer. Lean my bare back and shoulders against a giant tree then gaze into the canopy. My grandmother would shout, "Come back here, Lady Godiva!" when I would escape from my towel after my bath to dive naked under the fluffed-down comforter on her bed. If I felt it, I understood it. It was mine forever.

Touch guided my understanding of people. My father said he loved me. Well, actually he never *said* it. It was implied. Yet he hit me and knocked me on the head with his thick knuckles. He squeezed the top of my arm as he hissed warnings through unmoving lips. Presented with the inconsistency, my somatic interpretation won over what I was supposed to believe. A firm, unquestioned fact was formed, and I knew I was not loved like a child should be.

As time went on, the sensible world chided my understandings and truths and insisted that these things just *could not* be so. Because I felt the certainty in my body, I did not believe the rejections and denunciations. To satisfy the overbearing, intrusive world, I pushed the truths underground to a more private, safe sleeping space. All this information came to be deeply embedded in every cell of my body. Waiting, unbeknownst to me, to be awakened at another time, when circumstances would free them.

Marian provided the beautiful backdrop that stimulated my insight. And now, before the altar that was my table, I realized exactly what was occurring. All the latent memories resurfaced and were being released; I was at long last in a setting to liberate them. A reintroduction to my flawless compass was unfolding. My understanding of the significance of my unique evaluation instruments was crystallized. My hands had always been and would forever remain my primary assessment tools. My gauges. My guides. My secondary yet more dependable sight.

All at once, I realized what massage was to be for me: the vehicle by which the floodgates would open and allow me to again take in and interpret the world in a most truthful and accurate way. My conscious reconnection to the Universe had been initiated, and I would again and forever be free from the shackles of the sensible world. The pure beauty of this realization opened me to tears.

I began to weep with joy at knowing the Universe had not given up on me! I looked back and saw that it had continued to send me subtle yet salient messages, even when I ignored it for years. Calling softly to me. Sending me signs. Hoping I would begin to hear again. Circumstances and intuition had once again placed me in direct contact with our mother source. Every cell in my body instantly *knew* it was going to be a most remarkable sanctified journey.

At the crescendo of my epiphany, I was easing into the final phase of Marian's massage. A Highland rendition of "Amazing Grace" beckoned softly from the corner. I came to rest behind her head, slowly and rhythmically working the sides of her thick neck. Staring upside down at her beautiful face, I wondered if she was aware of the significance of what had *just* happened to me! Could she feel my pulse race, my hands quiver? Did she detect the acceleration of my breathing or hear the pounding of my now-wide-open heart as the energy from the cosmos rushed in to fill the stale, vacuous void? Could she ever understand, *could I even convey*, what was presently stirring in me?

All at once, Marian's eyes opened, ever so slowly and softly. They appeared profound and timeless.

"What is it, child?" Her voice swaddled me in flannel.

I was too humbled to answer such a question. Too much in awe to speak. Holding her neck and head in my hands, looking down at her with eyes purged by clarifying tears, I could not form the words to utter even the smallest portion of what I was feeling. The moment was suspended and sacred.

"Ah . . . I see," she cooed knowingly, clearly recognizing what had transpired. All the wisdom from the Universe reached out to me from her deep eyes. "You're home, child. Ain't it nice to come home?"

Chapter Two

FEISTY

The first time I met Mary, I was standing in the doorway of my office as she pulled up the driveway in a simulated-wood-sided gray-colored 1992 Buick station wagon. She got out of the car and leaned on the doorframe. We made eye contact. Despite the December cold, neither of us moved. We looked at each other's expressionless faces; nary a word was spoken for what seemed like half a minute. Suddenly, as if on some secret command, we both burst into hearty laughter. The fact that we began laughing at exactly the same second caused both of us to continue to do so. It took a minute or two for the zaniness of the moment to subside. We have been amused by each other ever since. It is no accident, I am certain, that the gravest message I have ever received came from a most fun-loving person.

Mary wasn't always this way. As a young child, she was verbally and physically abused. She was grossly mistreated and called "ugly." The horrendous handling resulted in the stripping away of her self-esteem and questioning of her value in the world. In her own words, taken from an earnest letter she wrote to me, she shared that "It took my stubbornness and the example of a gutsy, spunky eight-year-old angel to get the self-esteem train on the right track." She had a son who died of a prolonged illness when he was young. It changed her life, forever forward. She ended the letter with, "Prayer and strong faith resulted in an inner peace that transformed me into a beautiful person." My hunch is she always was. Meeting her when

I did, in her state of "heartfelt gratitude and deep humility," it was hard to imagine her any other way.

She is wacky. I liked to run my fingers through her naturally curly soft salt-and-peppery-gray hair. One year, for Christmas, she gave me a clear glass Christmas ornament, filled with the clippings from her most recent haircut, and called it my "holiday hair ball." She is zany. She had a garden in her backyard that should have been in a city tour guide under "Sights to See": interspersed among the hundreds of varieties of plants and flowers were creative castoffs from junk piles, other people's collections, and from wherever she could get interesting stuff. She even trimmed a giant bush to look like an elephant. She is nutty. She got her hands on a computer and pushed it to the limits of capability relative to humorous correspondence and artwork. She is unpredictable. She always wanted to ride a Zamboni: during hockey season, she somehow wheedled a ride on the ice-prepping machine at the arena. She is madcap. She saw *The Lion King* twelve times so she could justifiably claim to be the biggest fan: she finally wangled a backstage pass to meet and hobnob with the cast. She is off-the-wall. I was soliciting pictures of my patients who are featured in this book; she had a photograph taken of herself with her back turned to the camera, yet her smirking face visible in a hand mirror she was holding. The only thing that causes me to shake my head more than over something she did is in wondering what the hell she is going to pull next.

One day, I told her that I loved how crazy she was. "I am one feisty lady!" she exclaimed. She paused then, tapping her chin with her fingernail, added, "But you are feisty too!" She continued with her decision on the matter, "*I* will be Feisty I, and *you* will be Feisty II." Ever since then, for short and for convenience, we have called each other Feisty.

We certainly connected. She was much older than I—her kids were my age. Yet I would not or could not say she was like a mother to me. We were far too familiar and much too open about taboo things for our relationship to qualify as that. We were peers. We were equals. We walked abreast facing the same direction. At times, she was the teacher; during other periods, she thanked me for being so for her. We learned many important things about and from each other. Clearly, we were kindred, complimentary, compatible souls.

I met Feisty about ten months after I began my practice. She came into my life at the peak of an era, during an epoch whose time had evidently come. An age that when I look back on I want to smack myself on the forehead. Or writhe with discomfort upon seeing the truth. I was as brazen as I had always been. I was mercilessly forthright. I retained an air of entitlement. I constantly tended an in-your-face and too-bad-if-you-don't-like-me attitude. I was capable, talented, and clever. At times, I was a caustic hard-ass.

This information must be framed with two notable exceptions: Primarily speaking, my role as a mother. I do not only refer to being mother to my daughters, but I also mean mother to any child. I am unfalteringly attentive, aware, forgiving, and firm yet compassionate. I am a good teacher and interact on a positive basal level with children. My history as a parent is full of creativity and fun where my kids always learned something and didn't seem to mind. Secondly, I have always been very cautious to maintain professionalism and constantly strived to render competent treatment. I engage my patients with genuine dignity and respect and temper my bravado with sometimes-false, most-times-not humility. The mother I am, conjoined with my persona in the treatment rooms of my professions, is a composite of the person I always wanted to be. I was willing to place bets on everything in my grasp except for these two things. But outside of maternal and licensed realms, I flexed most interpersonal and societal rules until they splintered.

Feisty detected the dichotomy. Through some very pointed and well-timed questions, it didn't take long before she caught on. She told me that she would often refer to me in conversation as "my friend who flaunts it." Ouch. She would say to me things that no one else would. Things that, in hindsight, I am sure others were *thinking* but, given my imposing temperament and dicey disposition, few had the courage to articulate. Too bad. I could have used it sooner, but I probably would not have heard it anyway.

One definitive day, I was, on being prompted by Feisty with a provocative question, in exceptional form. While I worked on her, I related the history on the topic she inquired on, the circumstances surrounding the event, the dramatic proceedings that transpired, and the heroic outcome due in large part to my principled, unwavering style. I ended with the boldness that would liken me to a sequined bullfighter finishing off his quarry.

I paused, anticipating the conversational equivalent of a standing ovation. Instead, I was received with silence. Not comfortable, contented quiet. Awkward protracted stillness. I became concerned I had somehow overstepped my bounds. I offered a sincere apology, telling Feisty that I was sorry if I offended her. She did not open her eyes when she told me that she was not offended. She did not open her eyes when she told me that I was entirely missing the point of her lack of response. She paused. I waited. My hands continued to move as if coaxing a reaction. After what seemed like too long, Feisty slowly opened her eyes, deadlocking them on mine. "You have many gifts," she observed plainly. "You must stop misusing them."

A strange and wonderful thing happens when people are at ease and feel they are in a secure, nonjudgmental environment. They get comfortable. They say what is on their minds. They feel confident and protected in telling you what they *really* think of you. I've heard a lot of astringent yet medicinal feedback over the course of my practice, but this was a whopper.

It was a painful revelation. All in an instant, the summary of my sordid, ignoble life flashed before me. My body ached immediately at the impact of the invisible blow. As intuitive as she was astute, she sensed that I was hit hard. "I have offended you," Feisty stated plainly. She did not apologize, undoubtedly because she was not sorry. At any other time and in any other place, my response would have been retaliatory. I might have gone for evisceration. But not so with this gentle old soul. Uncharacteristically, I did not even feel myself choosing my words. They came with gentle genuine resolve.

"Feisty," I began gingerly, "judging by my internal response to your comment, I sadly believe you must be correct." I manipulated her shoulder thoughtfully as I went on. "The most important voice has spoken." She jested, asking if it was hers. I forced a weak smile. "No, Feisty, it is the voice of my body. It is the unanimous declaration of every cell in my body. Misusing my gifts is *exactly* what I have done. And for far too long," I concluded as if I had finally broken after a ten-hour interrogation. I was beyond tears. Even though it was "her hour," Feisty did not speak much for the remainder of the visit. She graciously allowed me the necessary time to let the pang of my harsh awakening begin to register consequence.

I must tell you, it is agony to divulge what follows. The thought of this admission makes me weak and sore. I've known it's been coming for months, long before I actually sat down to write this chapter. I find myself eating more food in an attempt to quell the unrest brewing inside me over the disclosure and drinking much wine to quiet the disharmony produced from fighting it for so long. It would be easy enough to end this chapter in some other direction, one that would not be so incriminating and one that might not cast such a dark shadow. But then I could never escape the feelings that would be forever harbored in my hull for *not* doing so. It is my intuition that there is an unknown reason and purpose for sharing not just this story, but also the entire contents of this book. Can you feel me holding my breath? Here it comes.

As a child, I developed the twisted perception that the world revolved around me. I always felt that I was entitled to everything. The biggest piece of pie. To be the first in line. Recognition. Prime opportunities. The best of whatever was available. I was not given the gift of patient parents who were able to teach me to combat my egocentricity. I am not assigning blame here—I am accepting responsibility. I truly do not think they knew what to do with me. I know that I was the toughest kind of child to raise. I was smart and calculating, resourceful and adaptive, savvy and opportunistic. At times, when they challenged my dissent, I argued and cajoled, begged and pleaded, pouted and withheld. They would generally tire and give in. My mind chalked it up as a victory. My body heaved a heavy sigh; it alone realized that I continued to gain nothing and lose much.

My mother and father noticed, as others did, that I had become a problem. They began the cycle of attempting to instill in this inflexible, headstrong child what they saw as proper choices, behavior, principles, etc. Naturally, I fought it. The choreography never varied. They pushed. I pushed back, knowing they would tire, as they always did. I remained stalwart and used this as a way of control where I had little. Eventually, I got my way. On the rare occasion I did not, I shifted into my savvy mode: I recognized the fruitlessness of my primary approach and engaged my more subtle persuasive qualities. Discussion. Rationalization. Dialogue. Conversation with one objective only. To have it the way I wanted it. I always wore them down. It truly did become a game. As the third and final resort, there was always the option to disobey. Which I did often.

I was *actually* so angry at my parents for not seeing what I needed that I lost respect for them and did not feel an essential life-giving connection. I envisioned myself detached from them, and this disconnectedness transferred to other relationships. This exacerbated the problem and unmistakably did not help me at all. I continued to remove myself from authenticity and credibility in most relationships. Because my needs were not met lovingly and willingly, I learned to scam and pilfer for them. Since feelings were not required of me, they were something I did not regard in others.

I began to see the world as a place where I could fool many people to get what I *wanted*, not what I *needed*. Much of this began as a method of survival for me, but approaching emancipation, it became my way of life. My infantile self refused to work productively within the mind-body-soul triad. My ego became a supernova. Being the least timeless and much less wise of the three, the spoiled child took control.

I would look around and assess any given situation, decide which of my talents to use, then exploit them for personal gain. It was usually very effective. I was the worst kind of bad guy. At least the archvillains of the superheroes did not make you wonder which side they were on or where their loyalties were. I would play both sides of the fence. I walked a knifelike ridge. I rode the wave. I relied on my redeeming qualities to routinely absolve me of serious responsibility for my actions, and I knew it. I perfected the sincere-sounding apology, and the only thing getting caught taught me was to do it just a little differently the next time.

This is not to take away from the truly wonderful, creative, compassionate fulfillments for which I can take some credit. The beautiful women I raised, the friendships that endure, the accomplishments of which I am proud, and the success I have enjoyed in my professions. Thankfully, I avoided illegal activity and brushes with the law and have managed to operate as a responsible, productive adult. These examples of altruism are difficult to separate from the backdrop as they are woven into the black tapestry of my life like gossamer silver threads. But then again, these occasional shining filaments are not what we are talking about.

Prior to the point of receiving this message from my hands delivered by Feisty, I was slowly scaling the sheer cliff of personal growth, doing well at progressing and evolving. Working in earnest with much effort while I held fast to the tenets from other messages I was receiving. An amazing thing happened after I internalized Feisty's admonitory advice. I found that when I shed the constraints I placed upon myself, I actually *was* the person I wished to be and portrayed myself as all along!

Is it possible to completely change the *way* you are without changing *who* you are? Can one go from selfish to selfless, destructive to constructive, self-serving to living a life of service? Can changing core negativity to positive use of once-exploited gifts correct the damage done? Can the Universe forgive me for near a lifetime of squandering the offerings it generously bestowed upon me?

I sincerely hope so. Since that pivotal point, I summoned all the strength in my body and took an inventory of my personal assets. I went to work and placed all my efforts on the positive side of the list. Where I labored to suck others down with me, I now work hard to pull them up. Where I used the breadth of my endowment to keep ahead in the game, I now use it to keep myself out of the arena. Where I used my body to chum, I now revere and respect it as the home of my soul. Where I lied regularly to avoid responsibility, I now speak the truth to accept it. Where I did only enough to get by, I now do more than is necessary. Where I dishonored love relationships, I now flourish in a monogamous one. All the characteristics that kept me captive when used appropriately *set me free.*

For those who do not know the pretransformed me, consider yourself truly fortunate. For those of you who do, I am truly sorry. Recently, I've been overheard saying that if every person I offended, took advantage of, or mistreated bought this book, it would be a best seller! The opening line to *The Patriot* echoes deeply in my ear: "I have long feared that my sins would return to visit me, and the cost is more than I can bear." I can only hope that the Universe is not retaliatory.

I am positive that people who knew me *then* are not sure what to think. Many are out there now saying, "Aha, I knew it!" Some members of my family continue to keep me at arm's length, and my ex still does not trust me. Questioning my cause and motive seems a natural form of protection for them: they have been stung before. I watch them regard me with reticence and suspicion. It is a struggle for them to trust in me. Can't say that I blame them. These relationships may be irreparable, but I haven't given up yet. I can only hope that continued years of sincerity may dilute a prior lifetime of duplicity.

Conversely, people who have met me recently, know me casually, or have only witnessed me as a mother or a practitioner might not even fathom I could have *ever* been any other way. I am uncertain as to what, if anything, will come of this. Whenever events are set in motion, one cannot take them back. I *can* tell you that I feel better now than I ever have.

After that day, I often found Feisty looking at me quizzically. "You've mellowed . . . You are a more humble, gentler you." Hidden in this statement was a hint of a question. Did she know the impact that her bold observation produced? I'm not certain, and it hardly matters. This one message, when heeded, catapulted me into the realm I was not previously allowed to go because I wasn't ready.

One person *can* change your life. One single message can force a cataclysmic shift in the method of your remaining days. Feisty did mine. For better. Forever.

Chapter Three

HELEN

My grandmother is dead. She has been dead for far too long. There are a couple of pictures of her in my dining room. One is of her on an airplane, sitting next to my aunt Betty; they are both laughing at who knows what. My grandmother is wearing a colorful silk jacket and bold earrings with a matching necklace. She is plump and radiant and happy. The other, probably my favorite, is a photo of her on a boat in South Carolina. My grandmother's back is turned, her right shoulder closest to the lens with her face glancing back toward the camera, her left eyelid drooping somewhat. Her eyes are fixed on me and are the color of the calm sea behind her. She is not smiling, but she is not unhappy either. It is the precise expression she would have given me if she had said to me what Helen did.

I met Helen about nine months after I began my practice. Helen's massage therapist of many years had died. While at the wake, she heard mention of my name. Helen took that as a sign and decided to act on it. She phoned soon afterward for an appointment at my office.

As I looked over Helen's health history, I realized that it had been completed with a fountain-type pen forming lovely calligraphic strokes. I found myself intrigued as I read on. She reported herself to be fifty-five years old. She inscribed "self-employed" on the occupation line. Not a typical response for a woman born in 1946. But Helen was not a predictable woman. She had recently left a production job at a big company to begin her new profession of taking care of people, their needs, and their situations. Young people, old people, and every age in between; her charges and responsibilities were as eclectic as she. Babysitting, taxi service, meal preparing. Errand running, house minding, pet sitting, elder tending. Caregiving.

Helen is matter-of-fact. She is to the point and direct. She summarizes most everything in an honest, no-holds-barred style, even if it means she incriminates herself for deeds past or present. Her assessment of any given situation is quick and accurate. She routinely dismisses anything above and beyond necessary aggravation or effort as "fuckery." Some might be offended or taken aback by such an approach to what have you, but I found it to be quite refreshing to meet up with another person who could be as easily misunderstood as I have been for maintaining a very similar style.

It is important to bear in mind that her forthright vision is not without a sense of humor. She laughs—a lot. Helen finds hilarity in the seemingly most humorless situations. Much of the impact of any "bad news" she delivers is softened by an impish chuckle and sparkling eyes. She laughs at me. She laughs at herself. She laughs at the persons in her care and the circumstances they find themselves in. No individual or situation is insulated from her uniform application of wit and humor. No one is slighted by it either. Somehow, she gets away with it.

For Helen, talking, emoting, and reflecting are important components of her massage session. It is as if she initiates topics and works herself through them during her time on the table. We immediately entered a deep, easy groove and found that shared concepts and opinions flowed as easily as the bodywork did. On many occasions, we both seemed equally as surprised at the similarities of our ancient as well as recent histories, with marked emphasis on common fault and folly.

"We are strange ducks," she stated satisfactorily after a massage session one day. It did not take long until I realized that I was interacting with a woman who was a representation of what *I* would probably be like eighteen years down the road. It was a pleasant sentiment to look forward to.

I refer to Helen as one of my "bell curve" patients. She became my patient when my practice was in its infancy. She continued on with me through the busiest periods of my work history, when it took a lot of effort and creativity just to get a monthly appointment on the book that fit both of our wildly fluctuating schedules. She remains my patient to this day, accommodating my twilight hours as a semiretired massage therapist. Suffice it to say, Helen is a good historian on the pulse of my life and times.

About two years after I got my license, I embraced an explosive phase. I was working six days a week, Sunday being my only true day off. My phone rang constantly with new patient calls, and I said no to very few of them.

My practice hit a tipping point, and I was slightly busier than I wanted to be. I was seeing more than twenty-five patients in a six-day stretch, baking a dozen homemade cookies for each of them, and still cleaning teeth on Thursdays. I had my two young daughters to care for and my home to take care of (usually in that order), and by my choosing, no cohabiting adult to help me. I was writing poems and short stories by the fire late at night because I was actively pursuing the prospect that I had at long last found true love. I felt myself to be strong, energetic, resilient. Prepared. Except, of course, for the inevitable implosion.

On that Saturday morning, Helen was my last scheduled patient at the conclusion of a very arduous six days; I was frazzled and spread thin. Helen was a great person to give this appointment time to because she gave energy as well as received it; working with her was a soothing way to ease out my workweek. I was glad to see her; I needed a jolt. We talked of garage sales and babies, about what Oprah said last week, and reviewed the latest "fuckery" involved in getting old. We always conversed the entire time I worked, except for the last ten minutes or so, when I massaged Helen's neck and head. It was then she never uttered a word, and I never answered.

Strangely, it was in the solitude of those moments that the collapse of the walls began. Mournful Celtic notes infused the silence. As I watched my hands complete loving ellipses around Helen's shoulders, I began to feel overwhelmed and alone. I looked at her beautiful tranquil face, and I grew envious. It was the exact opposite of what I was feeling deep inside. I was exhausted from taking care of everyone else, worn out from heaping on one more thing. Weary of being the solution. I felt uncared for, even somewhat neglected. I wanted to be considered, to have my needs met. I wanted to be held and told that everything would be all right. I began to cry. I wished my grandmother was there.

Helen never opened her eyes when I left the room. As she got dressed, I worked hard to stop the tears, but I could not. Too much had built up for too long. I was going to have to go back in to dismiss her with my face red and my eyes wet. I knew I would not get away without an explanation.

With a raised eyebrow, Helen looked at me as I reentered my massage room. "Let's have it," she commanded plainly. I started out somewhat under control, but before long, the tears were streaming down my face. I related my version of the crisis. How I was giving all the time. How I felt like everyone wanted a piece of me. That I didn't know how long I could keep it up. I stopped. I sniffed. I looked at her.

"Oh, *please.*" She put up her hand. "You need to stop *whining.*" I could feel the stunned look take hold of my face. To this day, I still do not know why I expected sympathy. "If you are anything like me, *and you are,* you will smarten up and realize that what you are bitching about is what you *are* about. You'd want it if it wasn't there, and you wouldn't have it any other way." I was staggered and unable to speak. This was where her chuckle and her twinkle came in handy. She smiled kindly and grabbed my arm. "You are a caregiver. Just accept it and work *with* it, not *against* it." She dropped her hand and concluded with a sigh, followed by her commonly applied phrase, "And so it goes." I smiled weakly but said nothing. I gave her a hug then watched the winds blow her down the street.

I thought about my grandmother again. I was drawn into the house by my favorite picture. I stood before it with my hands at my side. I saw my grandmother's expression and heard Helen's admonitory words. The similarity stunned me. Grandma and Helen were true caregivers, both maintaining a quality that made them so wonderful. Each entered the state of grace that comes with acceptance. They allowed that glory to wash over and infuse them. At that exact moment, I decided to take the energy I was using to feel sorry for myself and apply it to a more constructive pursuit; I was primed to acquiesce to what made me who I was.

We don't often make the effort to truly consider that *what* we are makes us *who* we are. And *who* we are often forces our own undoing. It seems overly simplistic, but that is why it is so easy to miss. Any trait can be an advantage or a burden, depending on how it is or how it is not utilized. Much of what we complain about is a result of an inherent characteristic that puts us there in the first place: an excess or deficiency in a personality trait can compromise even the most benign situation. Tempering wild extremes usually solves the problem. When viewed this way, it is easy to solve just about any problem.

In my case, there was too much of the fiber from which I was made. Yes, I extended myself to care for my patients and my family. I love to immerse myself in people. I love to help them and listen to them and care for and about them. But I did not nurture the instrument of my work—me—and the tool began to resent the job. It occurred to me that enduring this life is really all about girding acceptance with balance.

Acceptance is something that has always come hard for me. For as long as I can remember, I've held the jaw-clenched-and-fists-at-my-side pose. I would fight what was. Because I didn't like it. Because it wasn't what I thought should happen. Because it wasn't my plan. And I had the audacity to complain about it as well! I have now come to realize that acceptance is twofold. If I immediately accept what *is* while acknowledging who I *am*, I recognize that, in most situations, I am more than equipped to handle what is unfolding before me. I believe the Universe presents challenges to us in just this way.

This is not to say that one should be docile or fall into complacency. You can be driven by an unseen fire to accomplish a goal, fight a good fight, right a wrong, or pursue a dream. All are constructive methods of taking your raft, carrying all you hold dear, down the raging river that is life. You have the choice to simply throw your hands up and let yourself be led by the whim of the unforgiving churning waters. Or you can participate in the inevitable direction that the water is taking you, paying attention and paddling hard to avoid dangerous rocks, entrapping eddies, and stagnating pools. For in the end, we are all received by the calm sea. In one piece or in pieces. That fate depends on you.

Since that day, there has been nary a complaint from me about the situations I "find" myself in. I recognize that I am meant to be exactly where I put myself when I am paying attention to who I am. While living out my purpose, I have learned to care for the instrument of my work—myself. I strive to balance my pace so that I am not active in my own undoing. It is not painless, but I have help. Helen's words will continue to animate my favorite picture. Both will lead as well as follow me until I join my grandmother in the calm sea behind her.

Chapter Four

JOAN

We do not often see ourselves as we truly are. Certainly not accurately. Our self-vision is like posing before a mirror. After the exercise of standing in front of the glass, we are still looking at ourselves; the image is simply a reflection of the perception that we continue to retain.

Until someone challenges it. To see oneself for what we are, it is often necessary to be looking into the like eyes of another who has the benefit of an accurate outside perspective. This kind of feedback proved to be most critical for my personal development. It will shape the rest of my days.

Joan worked as an electrician's apprentice with my lifelong friend from second grade. He knew I was looking for bodies to hone my skills on, so he referred Joan to me at the time of my nonexistent practice. Joan was born in 1963, just under four months after me. Like many of the women sent to this decade, we did not neatly fit in. Our task was to question much of the position and choices of women present prior to our arrival.

Joan is thick and rustic and strong. She wears jeans and has her keys on her belt loop. She is very smart and has a sharp eye and a keen wit. Joan does not embrace girly things. No makeup, no primping, no hairstyling, no fashion-dictate following. She uses tools and has a truck and is constantly undertaking the struggle to earn respect and a place amid the world of men in which she works. The inroads she cuts are often questioned and resented—by both sexes—and areas that she clears are constantly being overgrown. Our form and function is very similar, so it will come as no surprise when I tell you I liked her instantly. Joan is just like me, except a tad more Spartan and a little more extreme.

She is private and guarded, polite and exact. I always had the sense she was keeping something important about who she was to herself. In spite of sensing this locked place, we became honest, habitually open companions. Both of us collectively could count on one hand the friends that were true; we added each other to our very short lists. I saw her once every three to four weeks, and I looked forward to the multiple personal and professional benefits of practicing bodywork with her.

On one particular Saturday morning, I was more than excited to see her. Joan reveres nature and the outdoors. She shares with me the belief in the sacred feminine and holds close many Wiccan practices and ideas. She is in alignment with the principles and philosophies of the North American Indian peoples, and her conscience acts on the sound premise that Mother Earth is her creator and her guide. It is easy to understand why I was so impatient to tell her about what happened to me the previous weekend.

Though I had completed my education in August, I was not at rest. Early winter found me precipitously preparing for and anxiously awaiting the New York State Board Examination for Massage Therapy in January. One of my former classmates, Duane, thought that arranging a sweat lodge ceremony would be an appropriate observance of the events. There we could bid farewell to a completed part of our lives while embracing whatever was to come. His partner was a shaman and had access to an authentic North American Indian sweat lodge. The group was to convene in Lily Dale, New York, an incubating community of alternative and holistic healers, psychics and clairvoyants, naturalists, craftspersons, and the like. It is believed that this nestling, cradlelike area of which the town is part is a geographic center of concentrated universal energy forces. A handful of graduates were invited, a cohesive unit of eight students who, by Duane's decisive intuition, told him would be fitting for and benefited by this sacred rite. I was very fortunate. I was one of them.

Joan was equally excited to hear of the experience. Neither of us had ever heard of a sweat lodge, let alone been invited to partake in one. After she was undressed and on the table, I entered my massage room. As I gestured to initiate the massage, she flipped her long thick red braid over the top of her head while commanding me *not* to leave anything out when I retold the sequence of events. My hands slid assertively down the whole of her back as I began.

I told her a classmate and I set out early last Saturday afternoon. We were to meet at Duane's geodesic dome home, share a simple lunch, then proceed to Lily Dale to initiate the two-and-one-half-hour ceremony just before sunset. While driving there, I reviewed the minimum expectations presented by the shaman. There were to be no drugs or alcohol, preferably abstinence from these agents for forty-eight hours prior to the ceremony. Though in an authentic Indian sweat lodge the participants wore no clothes, out of sensitivity to those not comfortable with complete nakedness, bathing suits or shorts and tank tops would be required. Each person was to bring a low-fat vegetarian dish to pass at the communal meal afterward, which was to be staged in one of the welcoming homes in the town. We were each to bring our own towel and a change of clothes; water for drinking would be provided.

I told Joan that on the journey, I was traveling light and feeling agile. I wore my favorite old jeans "commando-style" ("No underwear!" she interjected incredulously) and an oversized T-shirt with a sports bra underneath, Birkenstock clogs with no socks, and a well-worn wool shirt. In a small cloth sack, I tucked boxer-type shorts and a tank top to wear in the sweat lodge and a rolled-up old blue towel to use afterward. I carried a hearty brown rice dish to share and the summary of my wits to keep with me: in the weeks preceding the event, I had learned that the ceremony was physically draining and mentally demanding. The sensory deprivation and intense sustained heat were rumored to be difficult to withstand. It was my intention to experience it in its entirety. I would walk out when it was over. Or be carried out during.

Ten of us stood at the entrance to the lodge. It was a very low dome built from saplings covered in bark, with a hole in the top at the center. It was easily twelve feet across but stood less than five feet at the highest point. We all had to duck to get through the small door, and most had to crouch low while positioning around the shallow pit in the center, which was dug into the semifrozen ground and heaped with red-hot coals. I was drawn to a place on the ground just to the left of the opening. While everyone else was finding a spot, I glanced out onto the lake. I couldn't be certain, but I think the door faced north. The sun was just about gone. The snow across the clearing took on an orange hue, and the glow on the water matched the embers smoldering in the pit before me. The shaman entered last and, blocking the door, closed the deerskin flap behind him. We fell into darkness.

It immediately became apparent how the ceremony got its English name. With the door sealed and the lodge full of people, the temperature climbed very quickly. As if the heat from the fire pit was not enough, the shaman's assistant, on some invisible command, would enter the hut with dozens of melon-sized rocks that were heating in the bonfire outside. He heaved the load and dumped them onto the coals. The shaman would then pour water scented with various herbs and oils, forcing a heady fragrant steam to rise.

All activity and incantation was directed by the shaman. The ritual consisted of seemingly unending phases of chanting, prayer, collective utterings, sizzling rocks, and evoking waters. At times, we would speak in unison; at times, alone; and a few times, we were commanded to speak out at the same time saying different things.

Then there was the imposed, directed silence. No talking. No noises. No motions. It was black and hot and void. No concept of distance. No perception of time. No frame of reference. It was an inhospitable womb.

At one point, the heat began to overtake me. My scant clothes took uncomfortable hold of me. I kept my eyes shut to keep the stinging sweat out of them. The chanting from the darkness kept buzzing in my ears. My face felt huge from vasodilation, and I was thirsty. So thirsty. The ground had already thawed at this point, and the floor became a mud hollow. I turned to cool, wet Mother Earth to save me.

I sunk my feet in the mire up to my shins and could feel myself grabbing at the slippery earth with my toes. I sat back on the ground then placed my head between my spread knees, with the side of my face in the mud and my arms splayed in front of me. I pushed my fingers deep into the fresh moist earth, searching for relief.

As my body melted into the primordial mix of water and the soil, I felt united with the earth. I saw that I was born of and remained connected to the true mother that sustains me. I pushed myself farther into her, a welcome relief from the harsh pain of my existence. She embraced me in a timeless hold. For a singular moment, I felt my entire body temperature regulate. I softened to suspend myself in respite. The relief was swift but brief; the intense heat from behind pulled me back to where I was. I saw that I could not get out of this world the way I came in.

This is what a tree must feel like on a sweltering day, I thought to myself. I raised my torso and put my hands above my head. Cold mud from my fingertips oozed down the length my arms. "I am a mighty oak!" I bellowed into the blackness. "My roots in the ground, my heart on the earth, and my branches in the sky . . . May we all be like the trees!" I still don't know exactly what that means—I must have been delirious. Joan laughed out loud. I felt a bit slighted but lightened up quickly. I had to admit that in the context of my climate-controlled massage room, it did sound kind of funny, but it was exactly what came out of my mouth.

It was time for Joan to roll over. She told me she was jealous. I got her situated on her back and interpreted the look on her face to be a nudge for the rest of the story. I told her how four people had to leave the lodge during the ceremony and how the remaining six closed a tighter circle around the pit. How we periodically and sparsely drank tepid water from the same plastic gallon milk jug, but only when it was passed by the shaman.

How askew and upside down everything seemed. And most importantly, how I received my Indian name.

The shaman hinted we were close to the end as the assistant came in with the last pile of hot rocks, which he heaped upon the others. On opening of the deerskin flap, the embers surged at the rush of fresh air. I could barely see the round rock roll off the mound and fall directly in front of me. It hit a great stone below it, cleaving the smaller one into two perfect halves, falling open and apart from each other. Straining for light, I opened my eyes wide and pushed my face closer to take in the image. "Tell me what you *see!*" commanded the voice of the shaman from my left.

"I . . . I see a half-moon," I responded slowly. "A half-moon in a red sky," I concluded calmly.

"Well then," he replied definitively, "I give now your Indian name. You are Half-Moon." I released an exhausted smile into the darkness. Half-Moon. I slid the name over my head. It felt like it was made for me to wear.

I was done. Joan had been relatively silent up to this point. Kneeling low on the floor, working at her feet, I could not see her face. I waited. She was pensive for some long moments. "So, Half-Moon," she coyly began, "you have new name. What do you think it means?" It was my turn to be contemplative as I covered her foot and moved up her long body to cradle her right arm.

With a heavy sigh, my shoulders dropped. So began my monologue. "I was initially very happy about the name," I began slowly. "But now I'm not so sure. I've thought a lot about it since last Saturday, Joan. I think it is an important message from the Universe." She said nothing, so I continued, "I believe it means that I am unpotentiated, that I have not lived up to my true capabilities or promise." I could not purge the disappointment from my voice. "There are so many things that I could do much better and more effectively." I could feel my massage strokes becoming firmer and more intense as I spoke. I checked in with Joan's face to see if I was being too rough, then relaxed my grip. "I am half the person I could be," I continued resolvedly. "I need to expect much more from myself than what I have delivered thus far." A difficult thing to admit, even to the closest of friends. "The analogy is clear. I fear that the shaman has named me quite appropriately," I concluded, removing all conjecture from her pointed question.

"*Wrong!*" she declared. "You are way off!" She laughed. I was stunned. After all, how could she tell me that I was wrong about *my* feelings, especially when I was the one feeling them?

It was Joan's turn to fill my room with her voice; the overture she composed formed fast and fierce. "You are a single mom raising two exceptional, responsible women. You have a home. You have a respectable profession. You went back to school, completed your massage education, will pass your state boards, and start your own business." I could feel her skin admonish me. "Through all of this turmoil, you remain kind and generous and well adjusted. You are always working to understand and better yourself. The people of your inner circle feel loved and happy and respected." Her crescendo followed. "*That* is why the name was given to you. You move in your own well-distributed stability and embody moderation while flowing forward. Your whole being searches for equilibrium between your body and your soul. 'Half-Moon' represents all of these things." Joan's finale was flawless: "'Half-Moon' means *balance*." She held a satisfied smile, the one she has on her face when she knows she is right. I love this woman.

I stopped. I paused. I blushed at the description. It sounded like she was talking about a wonderful someone else. But she was describing me. And she was right. Objectively, all those things *were* true. Even on the most brutally honest of days with myself, the sentiments she expressed could not be taken away from me. I missed it. She nailed it.

As a child, much focus was placed on what I did wrong, with not much credence given to what I did right. It is no wonder I viewed the name the way I did. Much of the process of life and the people you meet in it are templates for reparenting. If you recognize it. If you choose to accept it.

I did. Joan's interpretation of my given Indian name forever changed my perception of myself and how I lead my life. I challenge myself daily to see my world and all the equilibrium it holds, not what it is missing.

In bed that night, I relived my emergence from the sweat lodge. As I waited for my turn to leave that inhospitable womb, "You are Half-Moon" echoed in my mind. I pushed my head from the constricted door. Sifted snow had fallen moments before I emerged. The brisk, bracing air received me and pulled my skin taut about me. The night was still. The quiet, deafening. I walked barefooted to the shore, knelt at the edge. Splashed the frigid invigorating waters about my face and body. The mud ran off, and stagnant heat hissed away.

I glanced down at the surface of the still waters and witnessed my clean, clear self. I glimpsed all that I was and all I could be. I set my eyes on a likeness that smiled knowingly back at me. Unexpectedly, my wide eyes were drawn to the sky. I posed wordless and in wonder at the half-moon above me. The power of the cycle of the moon moved through me. I was born that day. Joan's hand guided my deliverance.

Chapter Five

ANTHONY

I was raised Roman Catholic. I had no choice in the matter. I was force-fed catechism. I memorized the sit-stand-kneel-sit of masses that I was mandated to endure every Sunday (and on holy days of obligation) to keep my soul from charring in hell. Even at a very young age, the guilt-stirring exclusionary patriarchal posture of the church did not make any sense to the human essence living in me.

Yet from any collectively negative experience, one can still take away a useful entity. My appreciation for Jesus of Nazareth stood apart from the senselessness. Jesus, the man who lived a very human life. Jesus, the historical figure. Not Jesus, the myth the church has spent much time building by sedition of chronological fact—I have often thought how distressed Jesus would be if he saw what has been done in his name. One patient unknowingly helped me to revisit the impression I retained. I used it to bolster my healing, recover my self, and serendipitously assist others. I now understand what it means to become a disciple of a concept.

I met Anthony in the early fall of the first year of opening my practice. At this juncture, I was working part-time in a dental office. He was an 8:00 a.m. patient who looked like he had pulled an all-nighter. I found out, in fact, that he had been up for almost twenty-four hours. He just returned from a trip to China on business and had not yet reacclimated his body clock to this side of the earth. With a teasing smile, I asked him what he was thinking when he scheduled an early teeth-cleaning appointment immediately following such a grueling itinerary. "I wasn't," he stated plainly, with no acknowledgement of my attempt at humor. I sighed privately. *It's going to be a long hour,* I thought to myself.

Anthony closed his eyes while I performed required dental hygiene procedures. Most of his answers to my questions consisted of one or two words. After a while, I decided to stop my attempt at conversation as, clearly, he did not wish to talk. Breaking the silence filled only by the suction apparatus and the scraping of my instrument against enamel, the dentist came in for an examination. Anthony perked up a bit and began chatting about his visit to the Far East. He shared the phenomenon that while there, he could eat and eat and eat and never gain any weight. The food was so simple and healthy that even sheer volume was not an issue; in fact, he lost a few pounds while visiting for over two weeks. Without looking up from my chart entry, I interjected in my most deadpan voice, "You didn't go to China. You went to heaven." One more attempt at thawing this guy couldn't hurt.

I was surprised to hear a hearty laugh from the area of the dental chair, and I knew it wasn't the dentist. I raised my head to see Anthony looking at me as if it was the first time he saw me, a sparkle in his eyes and a broad glad-to-meet-you smile across his previously stoic face. I raised my eyebrow at him. I thought my comment to be somewhat clever, but certainly not *that* amusing. At any rate, the remark must have been my ticket in because he was rather conversant after that.

Now openly familiarizing ourselves with the other, talk came to my new massage therapy practice. "Really!" he said eagerly. He immediately reported chronic left shoulder and neck area pain and stiffness, for which he admitted having done nothing except complain. He asked me if I thought massage therapy could help him.

"There is only one way to find out," I said, challenging him to answer the question for himself.

He scheduled an appointment at my massage practice for early on the next available Saturday morning. As I watched him complete his health history form, I caught the glint of a heavy gold chain at the neckline of his T-shirt. I reminded myself to tell him to remove his jewelry prior to getting on the table but was sidetracked with a question and forgot to do so. When I reentered the room after allowing him time to disrobe, I could see that the chain was still hanging around his neck. I told him that I was sorry that I neglected to remind him to remove his necklace and asked him if he would he mind if I took it off for him. "Go ahead," he responded agreeably.

As I unclasped the chain, it felt lighter than I imagined while looking at it earlier. It consisted of rectangular flat open-style links. Judging by the wear and coloration, it had been worn faithfully for many years. As Anthony lifted his head for me to remove the necklace, the ornament hanging from the end caught my eye. As he placed his head back down in the face cradle, I raised one hand, allowing the charm to come to rest in the other. I found myself staring at a very ornate crucifix. For its size, it was very meticulous, the tortured body of Christ amazingly detailed. Around the entire perimeter of the cross lay delicate gold filigree, beginning and ending with a sturdy gold ring securely attaching it to the chain on which it hung.

When I see someone with a crucifix, I must force myself to assume that they are not pious. That they are simply displaying a symbol of their faith as they interpret it for their own lives, and they are not *actually* telling the world that they are narrow-minded and noninclusive. I revel in coexistence with spiritual people of any faith. The *religious* ones make me uneasy. I wondered which type Anthony was as I carefully laid the ensemble on the table next to the chair and returned to my waiting patient.

When I undraped his back to begin, I was immediately impressed. The fact that he reported the age of forty-six boosted my admiration. It is important to understand at this juncture that I do not mean pitter-patter-of-my-heart impressed. What I mean to declare is that I became awed from the standpoint of the perfect physical specimen presented. This man was cut. This man was hard. This man was ripped. This man had what I estimated to be about 7 percent body fat, which, for those who are lucky enough not to be preoccupied with such things, is *really* lean. Yet he was incredibly muscular. The first pass of my hands down the span of his lengthy torso was a glide down a silk-covered washboard.

At that point in my professional development, I was still learning my way around the body. Yes, I had taken human anatomy. Twice. I performed quite well didactically, and I retained good command of where things were located when I transferred the knowledge to my clinical setting. But I had to really focus on my training while navigating the hundreds of muscle origins and insertions of the body. I had to think hard about what was where and what lay underneath. Where muscles started and where they were going. Many times, while working on my patients, I had to close my eyes so I could see the picture of the muscle in the anatomy book and then transfer that image to the patient before me so that I could manipulate in the correct place and render appropriate direction of my strokes for therapeutic results. Sometimes, a thigh or a shoulder felt to me like one giant muscle mass. Excess skin and fat stores made the task of isolating muscles even more difficult. It was a frustrating yet mandated endeavor.

Anthony's skin formed a taut, revealing veil over his musculature, all of which was defined, distinct, and detailed. For a confessed anatomist and burgeoning massage therapist, working on Anthony was akin to working on a three-dimensional anatomical model. It was heaven.

I am not shy. If I have a question, I will most often ask it. I am comfortable with putting the onus of whether to answer on the person whom I am asking. If I have an observation, I will most often share it. I feel that stating what seems obvious in order to gain insight makes much more sense than lacking confirmation for what I perceived in the first place. So I took a huge risk. I asked, "You work out, don't you?"

Anthony responded that he did indeed work out. Daily. He even went to the gym on Saturday mornings for a light maintenance visit. Sunday was the only day he didn't exercise. His day of rest. *Yikes. One of those*, I thought to myself.

I avoided exercise my entire life. Sure, I would go outside and play as a child—roller-skate, ride my bike, play baseball and football with my brothers, go for swimming lessons, and play for hours in the snow. But I never appreciated the sense of exercising for the sake of doing so. The closest I came to a workout regimen was lying on the living room floor on Saturday mornings, eating Coco Crispies with reconstituted powdered milk while watching Jack LaLanne do jumping jacks. In grade school and even well through high school, I viewed gym class as a sizeable inconvenience as Catholic kids were not allowed to shower after calisthenics; the rest of gym day was spent periodically but inconspicuously sniffing the armpits of my uniform to assess how offensive I had become.

As I got older, I felt as if the edict to exercise was coming from all directions and was ceremoniously crammed down my gullet. The workout types seemed so contrived and overzealous. I viewed Richard Simmons as a caffeine-charged anomaly of normal human existence and thought that Jane Fonda had gone *way* overboard. The pizzazz and presentation of the whole fitness industry left me at arm's length. At the time, my five-foot-one-inch frame supported 135 pounds, but I carried it quite well and was blessed with buxom balance. I was thick and strong and could get through the day quite well, thank you very much, without sweating my ass off. I just didn't see the need. I actually went so far as to announce that I would *never* exercise. Very defiant.

I braced myself. Here before me was a man whom I certainly expected would begin the you-should-really-think-about-exercising and you-would-feel-better and it-would-help-you-handle-stress and pounds-would-melt-off harangue. But after he confirmed my statement of the obvious, he declined to preach. He lay quietly and left me to think. Wow. He had an opportunity to convert someone, and he passed on it.

The massage approach to his shoulder and neck seemed to help Anthony a great deal. A series of appointments was scheduled, roughly two or three Saturday mornings a month. The second time we met, I did not remind him to remove his chain because I figured that he already knew the procedure, but he forgot. Again, as I removed his necklace, I found myself staring at the crucifix before putting it on the table. At the third appointment, I entered the room again to find he had not removed his jewelry. As I went to remove it, I commented, "Someday, one of us might remember to get this thing off before you get on the table."

With a smile in his voice, he quipped, "I thought I would leave it on for you to take off. It has become part of our routine!" I chuckled, and for the third time, I unclasped his chain. Yet one more time I gazed upon the image of Christ before setting it on the table.

Markers that are placed before me by the Universe often arrive in threes. I have learned to pay attention when this phenomenon occurs. I am always surprised and never disappointed by what follows.

Each time I came to work on Anthony, I found myself asking many things of him. It was as if each time I put my hands on his body, I wanted to *know*. Something. Anything. Whatever he would share about how he came to get his body the way it was presented on my table. I was genuinely surprised to find myself actively seeking out information that, very shortly before and for my entire life prior, I worked hard to disregard. I also found myself being honest about the fact that the rigors of full-time massage therapy were taking a toll on me, and I admitted this to Anthony. Frankly, being a veteran dental hygienist was not physically demanding and did not take good aerobic capacity, steady endurance, or sustained strength. However, massage therapy, to do well, demands all three of these components. I felt myself facing a growing awareness that I possessed a weak trinity of requirements for the long haul in my new profession.

Now I come to it. It was not so much about Anthony's workout regimen or the program he followed. I wasn't concerned with how many reps he did on which weight bench or how many miles he swam in a week. It wasn't even about the fact that he clearly was a disciplined individual or that he worked tirelessly to continue to build strength and aerobic integrity to keep himself healthy and well preserved. It was about how he felt to my hands when he talked about these things. The gentle tone in which he spoke when he did. The sincerity and the genuineness of the content of his communication. His low-key I'll-tell-you-as-much-as-you-would-like-to-know-as-long-as-you-want-to-listen delivery. The response of his body while speaking his truth.

Touching Anthony while he elaborated on his passion and values made me believe them myself. Made me want it too. His preaching was not fire and brimstone. More a subterranean spring of cool water washing smooth stones. I suddenly thought about the figure on the crucifix. Viewed from the vantage point of my latent impression of Jesus, Anthony's gentle way was, in my estimation, Christlike.

I must make it clear that I am not suggesting Anthony is analogous to Jesus. On the contrary. I came to find out Anthony was a confessed flawed character, very similar to—though not nearly as badly behaved as—myself. In my above reference to Jesus, I am not speaking of Anthony the man, but Anthony the deliverer of a message. It *got* to me. What intrigued me was that there was obviously something in his method that caused me to finally *hear* what I had been blocking out so adamantly and for so long.

For the first time in my life, I felt compelled to begin an exercise program. I couldn't afford a gym membership at the time, but I started running and working with weights and strengthening my core. After eight weeks, I was a convert. After three months, a disciple. I was stronger and had more endurance. My breathing was paced and unlabored while I worked. Stamina drove me, and I wanted more. My body felt invincible. I shared my epiphany with Anthony. I thanked him. I told him about my previous aversion to scheduled exercise and how he was instrumental in my revelation. My life had indeed changed for the better and would forever remain a part of who I was. I told him that it was his Christlike delivery of the message that transformed me.

In the months following my transfiguration to a workout woman, I experienced some mild unrest over the collective events. Not that I was unhappy about my progression to better health. I was thrilled. But something was off balance. The best way to describe it is that I did not quite feel like I was "done." Clearly, I gained great advantage with my new focus, and I felt as if I had overcome a long-standing resistant barrier. Yet in spite of happy trails, my gut told me that somehow, somewhere, I missed something. My self-satisfaction seemed hollow.

One Sunday morning, I decided to take this unrest on a two-mile run. While jogging, it occurred to me that as a subjacent student of the Universe, I am routinely assured when anything of significance happens *to* me, it is rarely *about* me. "All right," I said to the powers beyond my comprehension. I put myself in an introspective posture and struck a contemplative cadence. I began work on deciphering the intended implication of my beneficial interaction with Anthony.

Back to the beginning. I got the message because I felt it passed through another person's body. But this was common knowledge; I already knew that my primary interpretation of the world is through my hands. There had to be something else. Let's see. The message was in his body. It was in his body not only because he believed it, but also because he *lived* it. Hum.

Unexpectedly, I found myself viewing my responsibility as a health care provider. As a mother. As a partner. As a teacher. As a healer. In all of these roles, imparting information is a critical component, communicating ideas is a pervasive theme. Did this divining rod find water?

Yes! The floodgates opened. Numerous examples of my life's proclivities came surging about me. I routinely demonstrate that I am a good teacher of those things I hold true. I *do* have a knack for getting compliance from my patients to either adhere to or change particulars or accept a new direction of treatment. I *can* extract cooperation where there initially seems to be none. By nature, I *am* very persuasive and have a propensity to get people onboard for something that is important to me. When I am acting on genuine premise, it flows. It is always easy. The recipients of my truths could easily hear my words because they felt them in my voice and in my body. The results, consistently positive.

I hadn't hit my stride yet. I was beginning to sweat. Suddenly, the swell of not-so-positive inclinations soaked me. I lied for myself and others to avoid trouble or responsibility. I expected monogamy in a relationship when I was not willing to reciprocate. I remembered the short stint I worked in that dental office where the hygienists were expected to recommend unnecessary work so as to meet the dentist's weekly production goal. I professed dietary restraint for many patients when I privately displayed none. At times, I worked hard to convince someone to do something (even though I wouldn't be caught dead doing it) so I could gain an advantage. I engaged in rote recitation of mandatory prayers in church while not believing a word of it.

During each of these, and I'm sad to admit many more, I may have been able to expertly disguise the superficial signs of inconsistency, but my body was not at peace with the dichotomy. I recalled the distinct ill-contented feeling inside me—always present but in varying degrees—following the transgression that preceded it. I believe this reality was transferred to others. On some level, their bodies recognized the conflict in mine. I was running hard now, getting tired. I was at the farthest point from home.

I turned the corner. My heart was pounding, but my breathing steady. As I labored toward the homestretch, the deep governing power that resides in all of us made itself known to me. A compass that always points true. Some name it "conscience." It has been referred to as ethics, morals, or principles. Code of conduct. Values. Yet these names imply that we have the capacity to *impact* this force. We cannot.

True, we have a choice to *act upon* the framework. Yes, we make the decision to be forthright or not, to settle on if we behave according to or against it. What we *do not* exercise an option over is the reaction of our body, our cells, our *very core* when we say or do anything that goes in an opposite direction of the plan of the Universe: this factor alone holds greater influence than any moment in time and comprises those miracles that are so much larger than our singular selves. We can suppress it. Deny its presence. Drive it underground. Push it so far away from our conscious realm so as to make it barely imperceptible to our mind. But we cannot eliminate this force. It is encrypted in our developing body from the second we are conceived. It will be there until the moment of our death.

My run completed, I sat on the sidewalk to cool down. The body may not know any better, but it knows best. It is a servant much wiser than its master. While working in partnership with the Universe, it is the inherent expectation of our pure physical ark that we will strive to keep our actions aligned with the purpose of evolving. Our deeds in accordance with built-in values. Our words and works to be consistent with the direction of the collective consciousness. This mandate is present precisely for this purpose. So that we may never be lost. So we can always find the light. So that we may always have a way back from however far we stray.

Oh my god. I sat there, stunned. I always understood this to be the single most important message of Christ. After my entire lifetime of sorting religious chaff, there in my hand was the very concept that stuck with me, taught repeatedly by Jesus. Astounding.

I began the crusade with myself. I worked to let my actions, my words, my deeds, and my work speak of that which made up the best of me and the finest human nature had to offer. I reeducated myself on the approach of letting my body—not someone else—quietly warn me when I was veering off course. When I communicated my purposes in the past, I didn't always *live* them—I merely *stated* them. I now knew that if I was going to talk the talk, I *had* to walk the walk. If I was going to profess it, I had to live it and breathe it. This is the cleanest, clearest way to get a message to another soul.

Quite possibly, another secret to well-being had been revealed to me. Perchance my new relationships are more genuine, and my old ones are on the way to repair because there is little contrivance left in my presentation. Perhaps I have become a more effective communicator because others see and sense in me the consistency that they are also subject to; *like* always recognizes *same*. I have more energy; it is not being spent on trying to suppress my body's call for redirection. My endurance for those things that would tire me has increased dramatically. I smile more when no one is around. I'm happier in my skin.

Since that Sunday morning run, my body has felt better than it ever has. I gathered more from that sunrise service in the outdoor church-of-what-is-really-going-on than I did in a lifetime of mass attendance. I, at long last, internalized the value of unilateral cooperation and consistency between my inward and outward self. I embraced the lode deep in my body and began to rely on that unseen wisdom to guide me. I put on the shoes of a disciple. I now walk the Way.

Chapter Six

RICH

Infrequently, erections do occur in my practice. As insurance against them, some of my patients have confessed that the fear of having one during treatment is enough to prevent getting one. The "mortification factor" as one man put it. I am unaffected and unimpressed when they do take place. The few times that they have happened, I accepted the reaction as a normal physiologic repercussion to stimulation of the skin on the upper thigh, the regions known as the dermatomes of the first and second lumbar vertebrae. My usual response when they do arise is, "Don't touch it, don't move it, and it won't cause a problem for continuation of treatment." There has been only one erection that upset me. Really upset me.

During my first few weeks of massage school, we had much unlearning and relearning to do. By no accident, I am sure, I started my massage course rotation with Shiatsu, a series of ancient treatments with Oriental origin. Shiatsu utilizes acupuncture points on the body, stimulating them not with needles but with pressure. For our first practicum, we started out immediately on the floor mats, paired up with other student partners. There were some same-sex pairs, some male and female partnering.

The lights were dimmed. Bamboo flute music whispered softly from the sound system. One student was instructed to lie down on the mat on their back. The partner of that person was to sit cross-legged at the head of the first student and get as close to her or him without touching. After a few moments, the entire class had positioned themselves as requested, and the inevitable mumblings that occur when a large group of persons get situated ceased.

Forty students, twenty pairs, all positioned in harmony, facing the same direction. Four sets across the empty room, five pairs back. I glanced around. In the dim light, we all looked remarkably the same, like synchronized performers in Tiananmen Square waiting for the single drumbeat signifying the start of an exhibition dance. The room felt still; every pair of eyes on Paula, our Shiatsu instructor.

Saying nothing, she slowly began to weave her tiny frame around and among the grid of mats and persons. Looking at each one of us as she passed. Her movements were relaxed yet deliberate. Just as she was about to complete her meandering through the class, she began to speak.

"*Gasho*," she started, with an appropriate pause that always follows something important, "is a gesture performed when initiating and completing an interaction." Paula placed the palms of her hands together, with her fingers pointing up and bent her elbows, bringing her hands close to the center of her chest. She bowed at the waist and, keeping her back and head straight, came to a stop about forty degrees from her upright position. After a brief pause in this position, she returned upright.

"This gesture represents honor, respect, and humility," she elaborated. "It will serve for now, as a reminder, to put you in an essential frame of mind prior to treatment. You must honor your patients. You must respect them. You will work toward being humble before them." She added, not as an afterthought, "You will begin and end every massage session in this manner. Those students seated may begin."

All the sitting people caught on at close but varying moments that they needed to gasho *now*. We had momentarily lost our synchronicity, but we all returned upright at about the same time. So far, so good.

"Before you may touch your partner, I must add one essential thing." She paused again, this time longer than the last. "Most of you will not have ever been this close to anyone other than your families or your lovers. You will be touching many parts of your patients' bodies with other different parts of yours. It is an intimate, sacred treatment."

She reminded us of our recent lecture on the five elements, which are used to explain, among other things, energy movement. She specifically spoke of the water element, which represents floating energy. Paula enunciated each of the following words clearly. "You must never entertain sexual thoughts while you are rendering bodywork," Paula continued to a wide-eyed classroom. "Your sexual feelings will be easily transferred to your patients through your hands and your skin. Your patients will feel it, and it will compromise the integrity of your treatment. If these thoughts come into your head, you must not dwell on them. You *must* push them out immediately. This is the only way to practice responsibly."

I swallowed hard. I glanced at my partner Jason's upside-down expression on the mat. His eyes were large; he had the holy-shit look on his face. Paula gave us the go-ahead to initiate the Shiatsu session by placing our hands on our student partner's shoulders. She began the process of walking us through basic Shiatsu positioning techniques. Jason was younger, striking, and had deep eyes, yet I would not dare let my thoughts wander in that forbidden realm.

Paula's mandate continued to echo in my head for years after she spoke it. Whenever I had any remotely sexual thought while working with a patient, I would immediately usher it out of my conscious space. For me, it was like the step-on-a-crack, break-your-mother's-back game we used to play as young children. I didn't *completely* believe it, but I wasn't about to risk finding out if it was so.

Until one day long ago, while walking home from kindergarten, I decided it was time to test the break-her-back theory. I stopped just before my block, looking for the smallest crack I could locate. (If I *did* break her back, I rationalized, it would only be a mild break.) I poised my little foot over the crack, looked around to see if anyone was watching, and definitively stomped my foot, covering the mar on the sidewalk.

For a moment, I felt nothing. I held my breath. My heart was racing. There was no detectable movement around me. Suddenly, I pictured my mother in the kitchen, arching in pain before falling to the ground, the fresh cookies on the tray she was holding scattered around her limp body, heaped on the floor. My exhalation brought panic. *What if I really did break her back? My father is going to kill me. What have I done?*

I bolted for my house. Ran as hard as I could, racing past a few surprised neighbors who were accustomed to having me stop to say hello. I was feverish as I smashed open the screen door, screaming "MOM!" while I tripped up the stairs into the kitchen. I was dumbstruck by the scene. There was my mother, standing straight as could be, holding my baby brother. My other two little brothers scampered in from the dining room to see what the fuss was about. I felt as much relief as a five-year-old could after realizing she did not, in fact, break her mother's back.

I stammered that I was hungry. I couldn't tell her what I thought I had done. With a knitted brow, my mother asked what had gotten into me and told me to sit down and eat my lunch.

I sat on the kitchen chair, swinging my legs while eating my peanut-butter-and-grape-jelly-on-Wonder-Bread sandwich. By the time the cold milk reached my lips, I had completely settled down. A subdued smile crept onto my face. I had done it. Proved them wrong. Came back from the edge. Beat the system. I would never be afraid of stepping on a crack again. The experience emboldened me.

I met Rich about six months after I earned my license to practice massage therapy. I was still obedient and compliant. Did everything by the book. Followed all the rules to the letter. Abided by those written-in-stone theorems dictated by the massage instructors and, like a samurai, adhered to them blindly and unquestioningly.

After a couple of years in practice, though, I developed the degree of comfort that occurs when something is done over and over again. Virtually perfected my work through sheer muscle memory, completely internalized my vocation so that I really did not even need to think about it; things actually came out better when I didn't. I became confident and self-assured. Instead of relying on scripted treatment techniques, I initiated a more creative, aggressive style to problem solving. I began to work outside the safe, known parameters. I embarked on the journey of questioning those things that were, prior to this threshold, untouchable.

So there it was again. Paula's call for constant vigilance. On this particular day, however, I was feeling cavalier. Kind of invincible. It was time to test the principle.

I looked over my schedule for the day. Rich was slated for an eleven o'clock appointment that morning. He would be a good person with whom to disprove the theory as he fit all the parameters to conduct such a trial. By general standards, I really liked him. He was a decent guy, smart and articulate, yet I had no specific attraction to him. He did not seem to be overly sexualized. I felt very comfortable working with him, never felt compromised or uneasy. He always treated me respectfully, both as a professional and as a woman. He was regularly conversant during treatment—no long drawn-out pauses during which errant thoughts might develop. But most importantly, in the more than two years that I had worked monthly with him, he never *ever* became visibly aroused during treatment.

So the fateful plan was set in motion. During the first half of a one-hour session, I generally work on the back of my patient, the yang side of the body. I spent the first half of the massage time chatting with Rich as per usual. In the back of my mind, though, a raging debate began: *Should I, or shouldn't I? Am I making a mistake? Why the hell am I even thinking of doing this? Why would I test such a thing?*

I finished the massage on his yang side. It was time for Rich to roll over so that I could begin to work on the front, the yin side of the body. After a few easy moments of adjusting the neck pillow and bolster under his knees, we picked right up where I briefly interrupted the conversation when I asked him to turn. We had danced so many times, we didn't miss a step. After a final adjustment of the sheets and blanket, I made my way toward his feet.

In keeping with standard draping protocol, I uncovered Rich's right leg, exposing it from the inguinal crease to his toes, then simultaneously tucked the linens tightly behind his hip and around the top of his thigh. Still involved in our light conversation, I initiated muscle work on his quadriceps, the long muscles of the front of the leg. After a few minutes, I moved to the knee, and then to the muscles around the shin, re-covering the exposed skin as I moved downward. I knew I was moments away from the line I was warned *never* to cross. My heart began to pound. A shallow breathing arc seized my lungs. I was a little girl again, my foot primed for the crack.

I knelt at the end of my massage table, Rich's foot in my hands. I took a deep breath. A slow exhale followed, one that escapes when, for better or worse, an agonizing decision has been made. I closed my eyes. Down came my foot.

As I kneaded his heel between my firm fingers, I began to think about the last time Michael and I made love. I could still hear Rich speaking and was able to respond appropriately, but the deeper part of me allowed myself to experience the music and the warmth of constant skin contact. I awoke to the infusing rhythm that drives my body through the hours, the pulsating fervor with which my fingers move as I work. I thought about the warmth of my lover's lips on my neck and the quiver of my skin when he brushes his rough hands along my lower back before encircling me. My body merged into a passionate cadence as I followed my daydream through to its natural completion.

Suddenly, I became aware that the room had grown ominously silent. All at once, I was yanked from my fantasy. Rich's foot stiffened between my hands. I sensed his breathing change. There was a tangible disruption in his body current. I slowly opened my eyes and hesitantly glanced up the length of his body. I was aghast. There, before my eyes, was a surge in the linens between his legs. "Tents" as we called them in massage school.

It is my nature to pace my reaction in a crisis; I have not been known to panic. It took all the discipline and control inside me to coolly complete the work on his right foot and cover it. I overcame the dread of looking at Rich's face. Gratefully, his eyes were shut, but I could see by his expression that he was unbalanced. I made my way up the table to drape his left leg. My insides were shaking. I hoped that my voice would not be tested. Rich had more courage than I. He broke the deafening silence.

"Uhh, . . . I . . . ," he quavered. "This has never happened to me before. I . . . I'm terribly sorry." He added exactly what I deserved to hear, "I'm very embarrassed. I don't know what has come over me. I only hope I haven't made you uncomfortable." He had yet to open his eyes.

"Rich," I said in my most sincere voice, hoping it didn't sound contrived, "it's OK. Sometimes, it just happens." I said softly as this was no place for my standard response. *What a cop-out,* I thought to myself. Here he was taking responsibility for my incursion into forbidden waters. But how could I divulge that my flippant disregard caused his arousal?

As we spoke of the horse on the table, it disappeared. The immediate pressure dissipated. By the time I reached his left foot, the linens were flat and routine. Our interaction, however, was anything but. The remaining twenty minutes of the massage were awkward and graceless. Conversation was forced. My movements seemed strained and unnatural. I messed with our ki; the sacred energy wasn't flowing easily anymore. I sensed common relief when the massage finally ended.

I hung my head. I was nauseous and ashamed. It was the first and *only* time I did not perform gasho before leaving the room. I knew I did not earn the right to close with a gesture of honor, respect, and humility. I extorted and exploited an essential treasure entrusted to me.

The hours and days following that session were agony for me. As time assuaged the sting of my transgression, I found myself focusing on the significance of what undoubtedly was to have been a one-time-only experiment. I began to apply this insight to a broader spectrum than the confines of my massage room. Clearly, it was possible to convey sexual thoughts through skin and hands. It can be done on a conscious level, whether or not the participant is aware of the capability. What the conscious mind is capable of, the deeper unconscious mind is much more so. If the transfer of such energy could disrupt treatment integrity, could it not also unbalance other potentially positive human interactions?

I was deluged with memories and incidents where I had realistically blemished or compromised a situation due to lack of control of my thoughts. Or times when I simply wasn't listening because I was fantasizing about physical interaction. Imagined a coworker naked. Coveted another's partner. Occasions I squandered the commodities of time and energy on fruitless nonproductive self-indulgent thoughts. Wave after wave of now-I-see-it insights crashed over me.

I realized with great sorrow that, for most of my adult life, I snorkeled shallow sexual waters in search of intimacy. I dishonored many and disrespected much. I exercised little, if any, humility. I used the gifts of my mind and my body as bait and trawled where there was no life.

Recognizing that I was experiencing one of those rare moments of painful clarity, I began to carry the concept out even further. If sexual energy can be transferred, it means that there has to be an actual *something* to go from one person to the other. When that something is created, it characteristically needs to travel and move. What occurs if the entity is not released, if it builds up or hangs about? Is there a sort of blockage or back pressure or obstruction that develops? How does the body dissipate it, and can it be constructively released?

In our society, we are not well taught to differentiate between sex and intimacy. All the messages we are barraged with tell us they are one and the same. This is clearly not the case. As humans, we crave intimacy, and many of us falsely search for it in sexual outlets. When the craving is not satisfied, instead of backing off and analyzing why, we go back looking for more. Other cultures teach that human interactions of any kind, even confrontational ones, are sacred. Holy. For the most part, our culture takes a hedonistic approach to things that should never be viewed in this manner.

We are taught that what goes on in our heads is our business. That it is a safe, victimless application. Many therapists will encourage people to have fantasies. To play out to completion those things that they would like to happen in real life but, for one reason or another, cannot. That it is acceptable to have sexual thoughts about that guy in the next cubicle or to ponder how good in bed the coffee shop woman might be. As long as you do not act on it. I disagree.

We have control over where thoughts go. We may not initially have command over a thought that pops into our conscious space, but we certainly dictate whether we continue to entertain it. To this day, when I am rendering bodywork, if an inappropriate thought enters, I usher it out just as quickly. I have extrapolated this technique to my life outside my massage room as well. I no longer view the sexual mind game as a harmless outlet. It is not. I confine my desirous thoughts to my lover only, honoring and respecting our relationship on a virtually cellular level. I cannot begin to tell you how refreshing and awakening the exercise has been.

I realize that this opinion may be unpopular and even sound unattainable. I must register what may seem like a preposterous challenge: a call for societal vigilance. I believe that we need to begin to develop the discipline to keep honor, respect, and humility in our thoughts. Like action can only follow. The change must start within each one of us. We cannot look to tighter restrictions for porn access or to the marketing world to step up. The solution is not in calling for someone else to change the horizon. Those things that are not watered wither. Using my experience as a template, my body tells me that one of the ways to begin to repair those things that are greatly broken in our society is to distill our most personal space. Is it difficult? Yes! Does it take discipline? Yes! Is it possible? Yes! If I can do it, anyone can.

I guess this is where I finally come clean. I never saw Rich again. He did not schedule another appointment. Shamefully, I never called to tell him the truth. I don't know that it would have made a difference if I had. I sullied the delicate balance that we worked to achieve.

The lesson came at great cost to me. Sadly *and* gratefully, it took becoming a massage therapist for me to truly learn the difference between genuine intimacy and sex and the sacrifice of this patient to have me *completely* understand personal responsibility. I once associated discipline and self-control with restriction and constraint. I now know them to be the surest ways to achieve illumination and liberation.

Chapter Seven

STEVE

I have come to recognize the healing that takes place in my massage room. I have learned that if the body is given what it needs, it can, more often than not, heal itself. I am a laid-low witness to the gradual deliberate process of repair. To the fact that touch girded by time is capable of curing . . . To the fact that I am simply a vehicle of Universal energy; the abundant supply of healing power works through me, not *because* of me. I never once contemplated the possibility that I would actually *become* the recipient of one of the most incredible incidents of healing that I have ever seen.

I heard about him before I actually met him. His reputation preceded him. While in massage school, I became close to a nurse named Donna, who was, like me, leaving one profession to follow another. Her husband, Steve, was already a licensed massage therapist. It seemed that once I heard his name, I kept hearing it. It was as if everyone either heard of him or knew him. His practice seemed legendary. I would listen wide-eyed as Donna told tales of his practice and patients, and I found myself yearning for my future practice during these engaging conversations.

For nearly two years while in school, I became very familiar with him once removed. During the inevitable conversations between students about treatment techniques and modalities, Donna would often share Steve's treatment choice for a given situation. The comment was always given broad due respect. The fact that, most often, massage instructors would agree with this massage therapist gave Steve great credibility. He even delved into energy work and alternative forms of massage that were way beyond the scope of most practitioners. I was certain I was wading in the wake of a prodigy.

Even after graduation, through my friendship with Donna, I continued to hear of many unique and unusual occurrences that emanated from the practice that she was now a member of. I occasionally worked on Donna, and because her treatment of her patients was much like my own, we compared notes regularly. Yet interspersed with our new-graduate realities were tales about this master practitioner, his peculiar situations, the sometimes-bizarre patients, and astounding outcomes.

Two and one-half years of work and actualities went by. Then one day, without a whisper or a warning, a phone call came. A phone call from Steve. Imagine my surprise when he stated in his message that he was phoning to schedule an appointment for a massage therapy session. With me. I replayed the message over and over again to make sure that I did not misunderstand the content. After numerous replays, it was evident that, yes, he clearly wanted *me* to work on *him*. I had to literally talk myself out of going into a panic. I was pacing the room, holding a piece of paper with the return phone number in one hand and the telephone in the other, asking myself things like *Why me? How could I possibly help him?* and, most importantly, *Why didn't Donna give me any warning?*

Finally, after a number of unsure moments, I decided to sit down and return the phone call. After calming myself and practicing my greeting a few times—"Hello, Steve? This is Mary Beth."—I dialed the number. I must confess, I hoped to get his voice mail. Much to my surprise and horror, Steve actually answered the phone. I told him who I was and that I was returning his call. He was looking for a Saturday morning appointment. Even though I had an opening that week, I mentally felt I needed some time to prepare. Besides, I did not want to seem overly anxious and wanted to give the impression that I was somewhat busy, so I scheduled him for a Saturday two weeks out.

During the conversation, I worked very hard to remain relaxed and to purge the nervousness from my voice. The ruse did not work. He asked me if the prospect of working on him made me anxious. I decided to come clean. I told him that I was capable and confident in my abilities, but that I was somewhat intimidated by a person who had, in my estimation, become somewhat legendary. He laughed and told me that Donna had spoken very highly of my intellect, my ability as a practitioner, and my pound-for-pound strength during extended treatment. "As you will soon see, I need a solid combination of all of these," he stated. I found myself smiling into the phone. "And besides,'" he added, as if it was the clincher on his decision, "you're a Taurus." Donna had obviously shared more than my clinical abilities. I accepted his explanation, and though I generally do not govern my life by the zodiac, I made a mental notation to be sure to read my horoscope for that day.

As the little over two weeks passed, my mood concerning his upcoming appointment fluctuated between acute trepidation and cautious anticipation. On the morning of the now-unavoidable day, I fought nervousness and self-doubt. I do not like to disappoint patients who seek treatment from me, and the certainty of "peer" review added additional pressure. I wanted to be able to cut it.

When I opened the door and found myself face-to-face with Steve, all of the unseen turmoil drained from my body. As I greeted and welcomed him, my mind was immediately released from the constraints that creating an icon had caused. I felt a broad smile on my face and knew it to be one of sudden relief fortified with newfound confidence. I felt strong and bold and ready. To this day, I am unable to explain how, all inside of an instant, the transition took place. I have wished many times since then for the ability to call upon the force that washed me clean of myself.

I found myself eclipsed by a large person, even by minimalist description. Steve was tall and thick and round. His head was large and balding, and his skin held a slight sheen. He had baby blue framed bifocals that made a bold, artsy statement, and he dressed in layers that only a thinner person would wear: he was ensconced in loud colors and a bulky textured sweater. In spite of his size, he moved quietly and smoothly. While I watched him ease into the chair, I suddenly thought of an active lava flow creeping down the side of a Pacific island. He talked with his hands in full motion and had a lilt of femininity in his speech and body language. His eyes, the most expressive facet of his person, appeared slightly magnified due to the lenses of his glasses. The enlarged appearance lent pizzazz to their already-dramatic movements.

With all this in mind, one might easily envision guided disharmony. This was not the case. With Steve, it worked. It all worked. He was pleasant to look at and engaging to interact with. On first meeting, Steve was a person whom one could easily label, in the fondest way, a character.

At the time I met him, he was sixty years old and performing seven or eight one-hour massages a day, five days a week. An incredible feat by any standards. Much to my satisfaction, I was able to help him with his low-back pain as well as other issues. Steve was very satisfied with my technical approach and felt that frequent massage would help dissipate negative energy he incurred during his demanding energy work sessions. We settled into a three-Saturdays-a-month schedule.

Significantly weighing in his decision to *keep* me as his massage therapist, he informed me quite matter-of-factly that I was surrounded by a luminous aura: one with radiant colors of blue, purple, and green. "You're a healer, honey . . . just like me. You're a healer."

Whether or not I believed them completely, it was my intuition to accept Steve's reasons and *never* discount or dismiss them completely—I wouldn't even dare refute Steve's claim to participate in telepathic conversations with Carlos Santana. With Steve, *anything* was possible. In spite of our significant size discrepancy, our bodies worked well together (as it turns out, we were *both* born under the sign of the bull), and I maintained the ability to drive treatment in my massage room while simultaneously gleaning much advantageous information from a skilled practitioner.

On a Thursday evening before one of Steve's appointments, Michael and I had gone out for a bite to eat. While finishing my second glass of chardonnay, I decided to take advantage of the proximity to a sporting goods store and stop on the way home to get a new pair of running shoes. I wandered into the shoe department, looked around, and found a pair of shoes that I thought might work. After placing them on my feet, the salesperson asked if I wanted to try them out on the indoor track. After holding a brief conference with myself as to whether or not this was prudent, I said, "Sure," while my body said, *Not a good idea.* I started out with a nice bouncy jog, leaving Mike seated on the bench with his cautionary look trailing after me. I quickly became bored running around the small circle, so I cut out of the shoe area, intent on taking a jaunt around the store. Suddenly, a large woman stepped out from behind a clothing display directly in front of my accelerating path. The look of surprise on her face over meeting a running woman in the outerwear section told me that she was not going to move. I stopped suddenly on my right foot and shifted my weight to throw my body to the left, avoiding an impact. As my steady course suddenly took a sharp turn, I felt a tendon slide where it did not belong and heard the outside of my ankle go *pop*. Naturally, the first thing I did after I apologized to the still-stunned lady was to look around to see if anyone else saw my antics. I was in luck—I didn't seem to attract any additional attention to myself. I hobbled behind a sock display to assess the damages. I knew in an instant that I had incurred a mild sprain. *Shit. Now what?*

I walked back to the shoe department, doing my best to hide my injury. While I told the salesperson that I would take the shoes, Michael delivered a wary look. In the car, I came clean, trying to describe how it happened. He didn't say much, but his expression spoke volumes. I knew that look—I'd delivered it to others many times. All the way home,

I insisted that the second glass of wine had nothing to do with my sprain, but I knew otherwise.

For the rest of the evening, I was quiet and sullen. While icing my ankle, I nursed my injured pride. I knew it wasn't a bad sprain, but I was angry with myself and still had making a living to contend with. I cancelled all of my patients the following day, disciplining myself to stay off my foot so that I might be able to see patients on Saturday. By that morning, it was very bruised and still quite swollen, but I could put weight on it. After binding it tightly with an Ace bandage, I embarked upon my treatment day.

Because I work in shorts, one could not miss the obvious addition to my wardrobe. Steve took one look at me and exclaimed dramatically, "Oh, honey! Whatever did you do?" I gave him the short story as I had already explained it numerous times and was growing tired of repeating and filtering the event. "Sit down," he ordered.

Dutifully, I came to rest on my massage table. He told me to give him my foot. He held my ankle between his hands and closed his eyes, pointing his chin practically to the ceiling. He paused, I waited. He opened his eyes with a smile, then looked at me ultraseriouslike. "Don't worry, honey. It's not that bad. After we're done with our session, I'll help you out." I sighed and worked hard not to sound patronizing when I told him it would be great if he could, but secretly, I became annoyed and certainly wasn't counting on a miraculous recovery. I was sure I had a long week of recuperation ahead of me, and I was not in the mood to play games or be mollified.

I somehow managed with only slight difficulty to get through, as is always the case with Steve as a patient, the demanding and difficult hour. My right ankle was very swollen at this point; judging by the pounding pulse, it felt as if my foot had a heart of its own, yet I felt surprisingly agile. I was able to lean on my left foot while performing heavy weight-bearing maneuvers and sat on my stool whenever possible. Aside from apologizing numerous times for "being so big," Steve was unusually nonconversant during the massage. I asked him if something was bothering him or if he was preoccupied. "No, honey, . . . no," he said calmly. "I've been focusing on recycling your healing energy back through you so you can draw from it." Wow. I didn't quite know what to say to that.

"I'll take it," I replied as I cocked my head, somewhat intrigued.

When I reentered my massage room after Steve got dressed, he was sitting somewhat forward on the chair adjacent to my table. "Now," he stated, "about your ankle." He ceremoniously pulled from under his lilac-and-turquoise ribbed sweater the necklace he wore quite often. It was made of gold. The pendant was disc shaped, like a satellite dish. It was easily larger than a fifty-cent coin and had a brilliant diamond held above the surface by three gold struts that came from the sides like a tripod. I had asked about this very necklace when I first saw it over a year ago. He told me that it was an amulet specially designed to concentrate and direct universal energy. He told me that it was a very potent tool. It was not for novices who dabbled in energy work, but a powerful instrument *only* for serious, highly trained persons. In the right hands, it was capable of generating great amounts of heat. "Hotter than the sun, honey, hotter . . . than . . . the . . . sun," he concluded with a raised eyebrow and much reverence.

After he positioned the talisman where he wanted it on his chest, he asked me to raise my ankle to the space just in front of his knees. I felt silly but considered myself obliged to comply. As I raised my foot, I held back the grin forcing its way onto my face. Clearly, Steve was very focused and intense. I quickly adjusted my attitude to one that was more respectful to whatever he was about to do. I felt as if I was playing along with some charade, but it seemed harmless enough.

When my foot was positioned to his liking, he leaned forward and placed his hands with palms facing inward, close but not touching each side of my ankle. The forward motion of his body caused his necklace to swing with a gentle pendulum motion, and Steve waited patiently for it to come to rest. Finally, everything was still. There was no perceptible sound or movement in the room. Suddenly, I felt very serious and intent. My eyes were wide as I watched Steve place all of his attention on the small triangle formed by his hands and the amulet, with my foot right in the center of it.

Within moments of positioning my foot, I began to feel intense heat at my ankle. Without warning, a profound quickly moving wave of heat flashed up my body. This was not a surface heat, but a deep, recessed fever that overcame me. As the current reached my chest, my eyes began to tear. As it engulfed my head, I found myself unable to take a breath. All at once, the building fire exited through the top of my head. I felt a subtle pressure release deep in my forehead as the last of it left my body. I was stunned. I took a gaping breath and burst into sobbing tears. I leaned over and held my face in my hands. The wake of the heat wave left me feeling deflated and formless. I cried.

Steve watched me kindly and intently as I regained my composure. His eyes asked me what I was feeling. Though I felt like I was speaking of *that which cannot be spoken of,* my response came without hesitation. I told him that I felt like I have just been given something. A wonderful flawless something. I felt humble and submissive and insignificant and small before whatever moved through me yet surprisingly grateful and peaceful. I heard myself saying thank you over and over again. I asked him if that was healing energy. Steve looked pleased. "That and more, honey, that . . . and . . . more."

Steve instructed me to lie down for a couple of hours and suggested I leave the compression bandage on while I slept. (If he had asked me to crawl around the block on my hands and knees, I would have done it.) He told me that when I removed the bandage later in the day, my ankle would feel much better. "Good as new, honey . . . good . . . as . . . new." I smiled and said thank you one last time. I honestly do not remember any conversation after that, nor do I recall walking him to the door or bidding him farewell. I went directly to the couch and formed my buckwheat hull pillow to the side of my head. Exhausted, I sank into a bottomless sleep.

Hours later when I awoke, I was disoriented, like when stirring from a vaporous dream state. The living room was still, and I could hear the kitchen clock ticking out the seconds as I revisited the events of the morning. It had not been a dream. With no hesitation, I sat up and looked at my swathed ankle. I took a deep breath and started to rhythmically unwrap the bandage, almost, I noticed, to the precise ticking in the background. As the layers fell away, my breath was deep and measured; I knew I would find my ankle, but beyond that, I remained uncertain of what would be revealed.

As the bandage end dropped aside, I stared in astonishment and wonder. I found myself looking at, to my complete amazement, a near-normal appendage. The swelling had left the joint, and the coloration of my skin no longer held the bluish purple hue of deep bruised tissue; just a slight yellow tint remained. My incredulous laugh followed. I put my foot through the normal range of motion, and it worked fine. I felt giddy as I rose to my feet, first cautiously putting weight on the joint, then testing it with my full body mass. "It's a miracle," I stated reverently to the empty room as I walked around it. I was ecstatic as I further tested the joint by standing on the injured side, picking up my other foot and jumping up and down. My foot and ankle felt completely normal. It was as if it had never been wounded. I eased myself on to the couch and remained motionless for a very long while. I needed time to process what had occurred. There I sat, simply in awe of the Universe.

In the days and weeks following, I found myself being protective and secretive about the healing: as much as I wanted to share, it seemed too sacred to broadcast. I have told this story only twice before now. The first time was to Michael when he arrived home that afternoon. He was amazed and in awe of the healing. We laughed together in faith of the Universe and held each other tight.

The second time I dared describe those circumstances was to a friend (who happens to be a physician's assistant) when we got on the topic of healing. Our usual debate of Eastern vs. Western medicine was lively. At another time in my life, my didactic "understanding" of the science of the body would have given some recognition to, yet trivialized, what my hands have always known existed: the deep mysteries of the human form and it's connection to the Universe. Those that cannot readily be explained but clearly do exist. This time, it was different.

Much to her surprise, I was now stoically siding with the ancients. Throughout my professional development, the more I performed massage therapy, the more I immersed myself in the certainty of healing waters. I began to use my clinical understanding of anatomy and physiology as a navigational tool rather than as a man-made map depicting linear instructions. The stars and the moon and the horizon of the body became my guide, my acquired medical knowledge simply a sextant.

My Shiatsu instructor once said that there is nothing more suited to heal the body than the human hand. Surely, she was making reference to the vast rich history of healing without the help of "science" for thousands of years. These are not anecdotal incidents that transpired periodically throughout the ages, but structured, documented, repeatable practices that have been perfected and passed down. Because they work. We all know and have heard of many of these, yet we roll our eyes and hum the *Twilight Zone* music when we hear of a healing through these channels. And channels they are. Acupuncture, Shiatsu, massage therapy, energy work, and related fields draw on available energy to work through someone, funneling it to someone else. Termed "holistic healing" avenues, many say that one of the reasons that miraculous healing is effective is due to the fact that the recipient of a given curative practice *believes* that it will work. They knowingly, or not, take an active role in their own healing.

One must not rule out the power and role of the mind. Not the mind that has figured it all out, but the mind that knows things have been figured out way before "it" came along. Belief that the benevolent forces in the Universe collaborate to correct and repair *must* be the critical part of the equation. Nonbelief blocks the abundant energy to heal.

Healing continues to take place in my practice. Alas, not spontaneous reversals, but slow predictable outcomes are interspersed with occasional, very surprising results. But is this not in and of itself a miracle? My patients and I have come to understand, even expect, that almost any complaint that plagues them will resolve in time: healing energy is suspended in our midst as we work and interact.

When I work, I initiate breath in my belly. It rises up my chest and out through my hands into my patients and back to me again in an endless circle of energy transfer. My patients know they are receiving channeled energy to assist their body in the process of repair. I know it is going to them through me. I know I get it back.

Healing energy is available. Try it before medication. Try it before drastic invasive treatment. Try it before going beneath the surgeon's blade. It is there for others to give. It will be present when it is needed.

I never saw Steve after that miracle morning. Interestingly, it was the last visit in succession that he had scheduled out some months prior. Usually, he would phone later in the week to set up another series of visits. He never called me. I never called him. We both exchanged a telepathic understanding: like a superhero whose secret identity had been revealed, he needed to evaporate. In my head, I heard him say to me, "Time for me to go, honey . . . time for me to go."

Chapter Eight

TRISH

When I was told I had a beautiful blue-green-purple aura, my initial reaction, of course, was one of being very flattered. How could I not be? Shortly after Steve made first mention of it, I mysteriously crossed paths with a few other gifted people who also complimented me on my colors. Numerous comments about this glow surrounding me came clustered and swift, yet after my surprise at the bundled observations, I became annoyed and envious. *I* wanted to be able to see auras and assess them. *I* wanted to be able to say, "Why thank you, and you have quite a lovely aura yourself." Why couldn't I see them? I took these occurrences and collectively perceived them to be a sign that it was past due time for me to get "the vision."

I have always *felt* the energy of auras, but never actually *saw* one. In the direct opposite manner as to how most of the profound seems to reach me, I somehow thought that definitive proof of their existence *had* to come by seeing one. Much in contradiction to the contents of this book, one might say, but follow along with me. It may be the one and *only* time what I felt was not enough proof, but then that was jealousy and ego pushing. I wanted it badly. I had to have it.

I began reading about and researching auras. Delved into definition and differing cultural and spiritual interpretations of the light we all carry around us. Learned of the designations and indications that the different colors of an aura represent. Came to understand the significance of the varying thicknesses and undulations of them. Gained instructions on how to sort an aura out from the rest of the visual stimuli grabbing our attention. I gleaned practically everything there is to know about this reported luminous self-atmosphere. I was informed, and I was ready. All I needed to do now was see one.

After many frustrating failed attempts, I rationalized that the technique could not be self-taught—one must seek out the skills of a master. It was then that I asked Steve, after one of our massage sessions, to teach me how to see auras. He laughed loud and full, stated that it was so very simple (honey), and that he was happy to oblige. Normally, because of my struggle, I would have been irritated by his comment, except that I was so happy to have seemingly found the answer to my lack of progress.

I sat down on my massage table while he walked me step-by-step through Seeing Auras 101. My instructions sounded very simple. "Look past the person. Do not try and focus on the space around them. Rather, allow your eyes to drift out of focus to a point just beyond their head. Take deep breaths, and keep yourself centered and your mind free." I emphatically stated that I had done all of that yet met with failure each time. Steve told me to practice on him—he had an aura so thick, people have tripped on it. I was exasperated, for after each futile attempt, my instructor chuckled deep inside his chest—clearly, he was amused and told me I was trying too hard! He ended the lesson before I was ready. I was told that it would come.

For about six months, no approach worked. I tried to convince myself that it didn't matter if I ever saw one, and then I'd weaken and attempt it yet again. I tried sneaking up on them. I tried seeing them when I was sleepy. When I was rested. When I was happy. When I was not. I applied the technique on people I really liked. Really didn't like. People I'd just met. People I'd known forever. Nothing. Finally, I acquiesced to this circumstance beyond my desire and understanding. I would have to be content with feeling them. I withdrew into a state of acceptance: seeing auras was not to be.

Many months passed. As quickly as the notion of an aura formed, it dispersed: I neither spoke of them nor were they mentioned to me. I did not think of or long for them. I was finally over the discontent.

Around this time, a new patient came to my office. I liked her instantly. Trish was kind of an I-want-to-be-like-that-when-I'm-her-age person. She was born two days shy of a decade before me. Trish was tall but not too thin. She had short spiky bleached-blonde hair and wore no makeup. Her earrings, small works of art. Trish's clothes were relaxed, yet polished. She wore always groovy flat shoes, and her purses were colorful and expressive. Trish was a flower child with contemporary panache. I thought I would know her for a long time. I assumed we would develop a cohesive therapist-patient relationship. I envisioned a growing friendship outside of the massage room. I had the inescapable sense that she would somehow be important in my life.

She liked to talk intermittently during her massage. Usually, we would speak of strong-women things, of good books and disastrous failures, of our kids and our past relationships. We would laugh at our mistakes and assumptions, then summarize, in inspired form, exactly what we learned from them. After most of our discussions, I came away with the feeling that we were both imperfect yet evolving beings.

On one particular day, a soft soaking rain fell straight down. I started the day with a smile on my face, knowing that the leaves would be raked another time. Though it was early Saturday morning, the sky had a late-afternoon pall. Gray was the governing color of the day.

Trish was scheduled that morning. Everything progressed through the hour in an uneventful and pleasingly predictable manner. I eased into the final phase of her massage. She was on her back; I was seated on my stool at her head. My left hand cradled her neck while my right worked her shoulder in long, slow elliptical maneuvers. I felt us breathe in unison as my hands moved to the gentle rhythm present in the mizzle outside. My body was engaged in a smooth overdrive while my mind was still and present. As close, for me, to a meditative state as can be. Everything was whole. Everything was seamless.

I found myself absently glancing down the length of her body. I paused. I was stunned. My lungs filled to capacity. I could scarcely believe what was before my eyes. There, forming a perfect perihelion around her feet, was one of the most beautiful things I had ever seen: a thick undulating fuchsia haze surrounded the blanket draped over her toes. As my hands continued to move in their patterned unconscious rhythm, I became attentive to maintaining the state. I did not change the focus of my eyes, nor did I allow the excitement building in my chest change the energy in the room. I did not want to lose this sight.

I watched in complete amazement as the aura moved about her feet. I saw that there was a thin colorless zone just before the magenta vibrancy at the outline of her skin. Following the thick band of nebulous hue came a diffuse, misty white fog that trailed off and became the rest of the room. After a few moments, I began to gape at the vision, and the aura began to wane. But gratefully, I was able to recapture seeing that which I was not supposed to be staring at. It was enchanting and enthralling. I was captivated. No description I could offer would perfectly depict what I was allowed to see that day.

I literally had to force myself to end the massage. I had another person scheduled in a half hour. I didn't want to rush Trish out, and I wanted to be prepared for my next patient, who was usually a few minutes early.

Still in a semistunned state, I told Trish about what had transpired. My eyes moistened with relief as I briefly recounted my struggle and eventual acceptance of failure. And now, I told her what I had not thought possible became so. I thanked her profoundly for serving as the vehicle for this gift. Her response was gracious and celebratory. She said it was very cool.

After the experience resonated in my body for a while, my mind began to participate in the aftermath. Why are auras important, and what purpose do they serve? Why was I able to see them now? Why did it even matter? Assuming (hopefully) that I could reproduce the same, what would I do with this newfound gift?

I've smartened up over the years: through my repeated mistakes, I have finally learned that when I am given something of value, I'm expected to *use* it for a constructive purpose, not to sequester or exploit it as I have in the past. I made a fire in the ingle later that morning and settled in on the couch with a cup of chamomile to consider the queries. I pondered these questions for some time after Trish left that day.

My thought process meandered along a gentle steam of consciousness. As mammals, we are social beings. We are gregarious and community-oriented by nature, *ancient* nature. Before we could speak, before we could articulate our feelings, prior to the ability to deliberately misrepresent our intentions or thoughts, we relied on markers to lead and guide us. Signs to help us navigate our complex social interactions. I came to the conclusion that auras are one of these very indicators. It was on this premise that I would bolster my professional and personal interactions. I would learn to use auras as a tool to assist me as an adjunct pointer to give me usable insight. My conclusion solidified and a purpose clear, I glanced contentedly into the bottom of my empty cup. It was then that I noticed the glowing coals in the fire just past my toes. I felt warm and wowed by the potential before me.

Over the next year or so, I practiced detecting auras. Initially, I was only able to duplicate the optimum circumstances for viewing them in my massage room (and at home with my children and partner); so subsequently, my practice became my study group. The more I engaged in this activity, the better I became. The more natural it felt, the easier it was. I shared my unofficial analysis with many of my patients whom I felt would be receptive to such a study. (To those whom I *knew* would think I had lost my mind, I never even mentioned it.) It actually got to the point where a few of my patients would inquire postmassage, "And how was my aura today?" The whole experience made me smile.

I learned that I was blinded to them when I was upset, preoccupied, or nonpresent to the moment and found that clearing myself usually cleared my vision. To do this, I would focus on a place deep in the center of my belly. Breathe up through my torso and cleave the building energy as it reached a point just below my collarbone so it could travel in equal amounts down each arm. I would close my eyes and place my attention on a point just behind the middle of my forehead while making sure that both my hands were in full, flat contact with my patient. When I opened my eyes, I would focus out beyond the intimate space I was working in. In doing these things, most often, I could see an aura that initially eluded me.

I discovered that a few people's auras were easier to see than most; those of others, I was never able to detect. Some had thick, robust auras. Some had wafer-thin barely detectable color bands. Shades varied, intensities differed. Always taking into consideration other factors present, I was able to, after a time, profile my patients and their usual coronas.

I began to integrate the vision of auras into the way I practiced massage therapy. Auras inconsistent with how a patient usually presented might clue me in on difficulties or low-energy patterns. I usually know if someone is struggling with an issue they are unwilling to share. I accept this without question and do not ask for confirmation from my patients, but it helps determine the *kind* of massage I give: a revitalizing one for low-energy circumstances, a comforting massage for those experiencing great sadness or grief, palliative strokes for healing bodies. Interestingly, my hands usually confirm what an aura tells me and work well with the integrated information. One of the greatest compliments given to me after massage is when a patient tells me that "it was just what I needed" or that I "somehow seem to know just what to do." After thanking them, I often respond that I am simply reading and responding to the markers before me.

Auras that are vibrant or thick or active or undulating clue me in on happy high-energy moods. Celebratory, euphoric illumination is a wonderful thing to behold, and I enter into a patient's place of well-being in silent festival with them. It is good for them, it is great for me; acknowledgement of another person's joy is an elemental form of gratitude and a basic tenet in the universal reciprocation of abundance.

Though I certainly find viewing auras helpful in assessing people's energy levels, I never rely on them entirely. When appropriate and, more often, when necessary, I quickly revert to my primary touchstones, my hands, for confirmation of what an aura tells me. But auras remain an important piece of valuable information that I use to be a more effective therapist. A better mother. A more attentive partner. A more connected human being.

All of this was well and good. I eventually became very used to the fact that I could see auras. I began to spot them around people outside of the confines of my home and my intimate workspace. I'm somewhat embarrassed to admit that I *almost* began to take them for granted. For me, detecting their presence became as natural as a greeting. But all of this seemed like dabbling when positioned next to the yet-unanswered question of why seeing an aura would prove to be important to me. This question was not answered for a long time afterward. The answer did come. When it did, it was very timely. Once, it saved me. Another time, it saved someone else.

I'm sure it is no accident that a small number of my patient relationships have ended shortly after a valuable commodity has been exchanged. My connection with Trish is no exception. One day, the wind took her. She never came back. Of all my initial assumptions at our first meeting, only one held true: I perpetually carry the now indisputable evidence of her importance to my life as I presently live it. But she has never really left my room. In every new aura, I see shades of the first.

Chapter Nine

SONORA

If you saw her pass in the street, you would have to stop and look for a few moments longer than a sideways glance. Any man might slow and turn his head to follow her as she salsas by, leaving any woman left by his side feeling transparent and woefully inadequate. The first time I met her, I had to consciously fight the feeling of being chopped liver. The weak part of me felt dumpy and blocklike.

Gracing my room at five feet seven inches, she must have weighed all of 110 pounds. I estimated the lower half of her to be a size 2, supporting a slight torso with enormous breasts. She had shimmering jet-black hair that fell seductively to her small shoulders. Big deep hazel-green eyes. Her complexion appeared to have a flawless matte finish, with just the right amount of pink tingeing her high cheekbones. Slender waiflike arms ended in small hands with long perfectly french-manicured nails. Endless legs accented by size 6 high-heel pumps. Her clothes were sexy, bordering on being tasteful. She even smelled rich and luscious. You get the picture.

After initial introductions, I offered her a seat in the chair opposite my massage table. I asked her to complete a health history form, which was handed her on a clear blue acrylic clipboard. I sat quietly on my massage table as she dutifully crossed her legs and reached for the pen to begin the task. As I watched her, I thought it strange that she had to go through numerous manipulations, working intently around her very long fingernails to get the clipboard positioned correctly. Sonora held the pen in a very unnatural position to get her words on to the paper. I suddenly thought of the time I dressed up as Elvira for a Halloween costume party. I placed long black press-on nails over my own very short ones. As Sonora filled out her form, my hands remembered how difficult it was to do anything. Eating was a challenge, holding my wineglass proved to be a problem. Adjusting my costume, scratching under my itchy bodice, reapplying black lipstick—each took much more effort than would normally be needed. I even had to ask my friend Sue to come into the bathroom stall with me to pull up my fishnets after I was done peeing. Gratefully, we both had a few glasses of wine prior. Now *there* is a true friend. Yikes!

She smiled and delicately handed the clipboard back to me, flashing perfect white teeth. I smiled back while noticing a furrow on her forehead between her eyebrows. I worked hard not to stare at her face; there would be plenty of time to do that when she was on the table with her eyes closed.

Sonora listed her primary complaint as upper—and low-back pain, along with chronic discomfort in her legs and forearms. She had been to the chiropractor for numerous adjustments and was told that her spinal alignment was quite good and that she was most likely experiencing muscle pain. So came the referral for massage therapy to determine if her pain could be managed through muscle decompression and manipulation.

This all seemed rather mysterious to me until I read farther down her health form. Approximately ten months prior, she had undergone breast augmentation surgery. On questioning her about the procedure, I found that she went from her initial natural 34B size to wearing a 40D (as in Damn!) bra. I asked her if it had occurred to her that the additional weight out in front could be contributory to her current problems with her back, neck, and appendages. She stared at me, looking somewhat surprised. "Do you think that is what's causing my problem?"

"Perhaps," I said aloud. *Absolutely,* I said in my head, now *knowing* that this was the reason.

I spoke briefly about pelvic biomechanics and posture and weight distribution. I explained that the fulcrum of the body is low in the belly, deep in the hip bones. That most often, a body is genetically determined to be proportionate to the pelvis relative to spinal column length, rib cage size, appendage length, and healthy body weight for frame size. Every once in a while, the proportion is off, either naturally or due to some external factor. Any great deviation from these external and internal proportions causes dysfunction and/or stress of the muscle and nervous systems that animate the skeleton. I told her that some women actually have breast reduction to alleviate the chronic muscle and skeletal pain that being "top-heavy" causes.

"Having breast augmentation may actually be the reason for your complaints," I concluded, working not to sound judgmental. "I can give you more feedback when I start working on your muscles." As I reviewed the remainder of her form, I found myself cursing the chiropractor for not having the balls to tell her that her new breasts were the problem.

I ran her through the paces for getting on the massage table. When I told her that she needed to start out on her stomach with her face in the cradle, she stared at me blankly. She explained that she could not *possibly* lie on her stomach comfortably. I told her that when I came back into the room, I would bring some additional linens and pillows to bolster her chest so that she could tolerate the position and that while waiting for me to reenter, she could prop herself up on her elbows and forearms. As I left the room, I felt myself already becoming drained from this massage, and it hadn't even started.

It took a few awkward moments of attempting to get her to lie comfortably without compromising her privacy or dignity. I managed to position the face cradle back and high, roll towels under her rib cage and across her collarbone, and raise the armrest to accommodate the distance of her forearms from it. When we finally got it right, Sonora exhaled a deep sigh.

"I haven't been on my stomach like this in almost a year. I used to sleep like this all the time," she said longingly. "I'd forgotten how good it feels. I didn't realize how much my body has missed it," her voice trailed off as I undraped her back to begin the massage. As I pumped gel into my hands and warmed them to begin, her observation stuck with me, hovering curiously close to the part of my brain that makes connections to seemingly unrelated entities. I could feel it hanging there, waiting for something else to attach to it.

I had a great deal of difficulty finding a flow with Sonora. Never really did get a groove. She had, what seemed at the time, a strange way of tensing up just as I made my way in. When I began to achieve some success with the high muscles of the back of her neck, I felt her harden under my fingers. When I asked if everything was OK, she mentioned that she just had her hair colored and styled and asked if I would please not get too far onto her head. I was asked not to work on her face as it would smudge her makeup, and it might make her skin break out. I suggested that she close her eyes and try to relax. Alas, she could not—her contacts made her eyes very sore and dry if she closed them for too long. My attempt to initiate massage on her belly was halted with stiff abdominal muscles: would I please not work on her stomach—she was very conscious of the few pounds she had put on . . . *where?* While I was working on her feet, again, she tightened up, wondering if the oils in my gel would affect the finish of her toenail polish. Her bikini area had recently been waxed, so I was to avoid the top part of her leg where the crease forms at the body. I was asked to be careful of the skin below her collarbone as it was tight due to the weight of her breasts. Numerous other restrictions followed.

It seemed that every place on her body that I needed to go, there was an instruction, a caution, a stipulation for proceeding; or I was shut out completely. It reminded me of the scene from the movie *Young Frankenstein* where Madeline Kahn was saying goodbye to Gene Wilder at the train station. As he tried to kiss her, she wouldn't let him touch her hair or her nails or her face or her dress for fear that he would mess them up. (Taffeta, darling!) They ended up rubbing elbows to say farewell.

Sonora's body felt very tightly wound. It had a peculiar undercurrent of tension that I had felt before, but at the time, I couldn't identify where or when. I was agitated and off-center, and found myself wanting the massage to be over. Imagine my surprise when Sonora told me that it felt wonderful and that she would like to schedule another appointment. Anyone watching would have thought we both had a hard time with the session.

As I finished forcing my hands around her tiny troubled body, I began to realize that I had jumped to quite an unreliable conclusion. It took the entire hour of listening with my hands to her body's revealing discourse to put it all together. It slowly occurred to me that the new breasts were not the entire problem. They were simply the straw that broke the beauty's back.

At subsequent visits, I was able to learn a bit more and confirm my theory on Sonora's difficulties. It started out as a slow seduction—as it always does when we give ourselves away one small piece at a time. Sonora stated that though she was always very pretty, she confessed to having a bit of a self-esteem problem. She found that in her teen years, if she put on makeup and wore certain clothing, she was the envy of most girls and the center of attention of all boys. She decided to forgo college to build a life and living around her physical presence and sought the latest and greatest ways to "accentuate" her natural good looks. After some mediocre photo shoots with marginal results and low-scale modeling jobs, she found herself at twenty-six working for a wholesale liquor company in an outside sales position. It was here that the real trouble started.

Apparently, the end-product liquor business is very competitive. It is mainly a male-run industry. Men own a high percentage of liquor stores, restaurants, and bars and are buyers for these establishments. There are many gifts and incentives. There are kickbacks and perks. There are many angles to exploit relative to sales. Sonora found one. It was here that she did very well.

Sonora was an immediate hit. A cold call to a liquor store would result in instant attention and a subsequent order. An unscheduled stop at a bar would end up in a sale. Handing her card to the manager of a restaurant would materialize into a scheduled appointment to evaluate stock and place an order. She reached top sales for the company in her first year. Sonora surpassed her own record the second year. She was tens of thousands of dollars in sales above the closest salesman behind her. Her social life wasn't lacking for anything, either. She was on fire, and she was hot.

But every fire dies down. Though still quite high, her numbers dipped in the third year. She confessed to not wanting to accept the reality that the novelty of her presence seemed to be wearing off and felt that "getting old" was part of the problem. She turned to the only thing she knew to stoke the flame—she sought more and more ways to keep herself looking youthful and worthy of attention, ensuring that commerce would continue to be shunted her way: Higher shoes. Bolder hair color. More radiant makeup. Tighter clothes. Longer nails. A more stringent workout regimen.

Though much energy and money was being expended to keep the illusion alive, things started to taper off after a profitable seven-year run. Sonora decided to take a hefty chunk of her sales commissions and have her breasts enlarged. Ten months later, she found her way to my office, miserable and in much discomfort, looking for relief.

As I finished our third session, it was obvious that though massage therapy was helping slake the chronic muscle pain, it was not addressing what I assessed as the root cause. I knew I needed to have a difficult conversation with Sonora. It would prove to be the last time we worked together.

I told her that I could not, in good conscience, treat her if I was not completely honest in my evaluation of the situation. I told her that massage was only treating the symptoms, not what I saw as the cause of her pain. I reported that I felt that much of the new muscle and skeletal pain was due to the breast enlargements though a good portion of the chronic strain she was feeling was due to all the incremental "improvements" she had learned to endure over the years. I felt as if I was giving her a terminal diagnosis when I told her that the consistent discomfort she felt could be greatly reduced if she was willing to consider breast reduction. That if she stopped wearing high heels five days a week, she would feel relief with or without another breast surgery. That if she stripped her daily self down to a just a few beauty buttresses, her body would begin to rebound. Would relearn how to be comfortable again. Would begin to dissipate the chronic stress. Reducing these physical restraints would mitigate the passageway for comfort.

"You don't need all of these trappings, Sonora," I concluded, placing my hand on hers. "You are an incredibly beautiful woman. Your body would be more comfortable if you would just allow it to speak for itself."

Sonora's response to my assessment was tearful and sincere and just about broke my heart. She responded that she had probably known this on some level. That it had been getting harder and harder to force herself into her costume every morning, day in and day out. Her eyes pooled as she somberly stated that the chronic pain was wearing her down, but that she saw no other option but to continue on her chosen path. There she sat with her chest heaving, mascara running down her now-ruddy cheeks, a portion of her hair stuck way out of place.

"I cannot bear to be seen without those things I have come to rely on," she concluded, sounding defeated. "I don't have the courage."

Sonora stood. She delicately dried the last tear with the edge of her perfect pinky finger. She thanked me for my time. She said she would call for her next appointment. I knew this was a lie. I would never see her again.

The human body needs to move freely through space and time. The proportions of our body have developed over millions of years of evolution; our erect level-footed posture is the preferred neutral position from which efficient maneuverability, motion, and function initiate. The unencumbered skeletal, muscular, and neurological as well as other body systems work in harmony to animate us in a very fluid, virtually effortless way.

At times, nature does not completely cooperate with the ideal blueprint. One leg may be longer than the other, a foot may have developed with no toes, a spine may have an extra curve, or some other developmental disproportion or anomaly occurs. In these cases, there are various corrective or constructive things that can be done to get the body back to as close to neutral as possible, given the limitation. Special shoes can be made for leg-length discrepancy or lack of toes, braces or specialized physical therapy can be utilized for spinal misalignments, for example. In all cases of deviation from ideal, the concept is to make every attempt to reestablish neutral position so that the body can feel better and function optimally.

Functioning optimally does not just mean moving fluidly, getting through the day without undue fatigue, falling asleep easily, or adjusting without injury to a change in terrain. It also means being able to handle tension, digest your food properly, react to changes in environment or temperature, manage emotions, and maintain a centered calm. It means being able to keep your wits about you.

Any constraint or restraint, any external contrivance or influence placed upon the body, takes a certain amount of energy away from metabolic processes. It may be only a small amount, it may be a large value, but it is taken away. The body interprets this menace and exchanges it to one currency only: stress. Anything that challenges the neutral form causes somatic strain. The systems of the body must react. Must compensate. Must offset. Must balance the offending entity and work to get the entire biomechanical system back to neutral. It takes energy getting there. It takes energy staying there. Less energy for metabolic processes. Less energy for maintenance. Less energy for homeostasis. Less energy for life. For any habitual or permanent change for the worse in the system, the body must shunt that amount of energy every day, all day, toward compensation for the trauma. And make no mistake, trauma it is.

When you decide to relax, do you first put on your dressiest outfit? Do you force your feet into high heels to clean the garage or go for a walk? Do men put on a tie when they wake on their day off, then sit down to read the paper? Do we put on our makeup and coif our hair before we bum around on a Saturday morning? Of course not. When our body is comfortable, we are comfortable. Why do we love our sweats? Why is "Casual Friday" everyone's favorite day to get dressed for work? Why is it that the first thing we do when we get home from anywhere "out" is to put on easy garments? Because it gives our body the go-ahead to be itself, allows it to function in the state it loves most: unencumbered natural existence.

Women appear to heap upon the body either incremental or profound difficulties and seem to actually go out of their way to make it complicated for the body to function simply. Hair so perfect that you cannot run extemporaneous fingers through it or unaffectedly go out in bad weather. A made-up face that must be protected from being smudged. Fake nails challenging digital manipulation. Wrinkle-eliminating chemical injections that decrease facial expression. Forcing of the intricately fitted bones of the feet into ridiculous shoes, putting them in absurd positions before asking them to support the full weight of the body. Restrictive tight-fitting clothing. Starving the body with fad diets. Putting bleach in the mouth to whiten teeth. Waxing. Perpetual tanning. Contacts. Butt lifts. Face-lifts. New breasts. The list is endless. So is the strain on the body, which ultimately must bear the brunt of the abuse.

Compared with how most of us choose to travel through our days, the chronicle of Sonora resides in the outer reaches of the extreme. Paradoxically, we can often find temperance through witnessing excessiveness. I am not suggesting that we eliminate the aforementioned entities or ban the use of those things that put some strain on our bodies. At times, I am tempted to place restraints upon my body; sometimes, I give in. I wear heels once in a while. Every so often, I'll strut or primp or subject my body to less-than-comfortable clothing. Fortunately, any stable system can rebound from an occasional assault. That is part of the beauty of the body's design. The key is in the frequency.

Sonora is an unnatural beauty. I see her as my most tragic patient. Thirty-four years old and most likely confined for the rest of her life in the exoskeletal prison she created, costing much money, effort, and *energy* for ongoing construction and maintenance. Squandering and squeezing out every last bit of metabolic energy on window dressing. Forcing her beautiful form to operate bound and gagged. Diverting the energy needed to achieve relaxation, serenity, awareness, and, quite possibly, enlightenment. How heartbreaking that she holds in her hand the key to the cell she stares from, but it is left unused. She has grown dependent on wearing iron bars.

Chapter Ten

AMERITHERM

On this unusual morning, the normal waking wave at my house was choppy, with a not-so-subtle undercurrent. I smelled a storm coming, could feel myself fighting to keep the rising tide from touching me. I knew I needed some extra time to center myself before what always proved to be a demanding day. The thirty-minute drive was opportune, so I shoved off at about 6:40 a.m., earlier than usual, for Ameritherm.

By the time I got off the interstate, I was serene. I headed south on Route 383 and began the fifteen-mile meandering pastoral route to the company in Scottsville where I had been contracting massage therapy every other Friday for six years. Now that I was traveling only about forty miles per hour, I rolled my window down to catch some of the refreshing air on my face. It had been a steamy evening the night before. Never even cooled off enough to want to slide my light blanket up over my exposed shoulder skin. It was actually hotter in the deep of the night than it was in the fine mist of the early morn.

I inhaled the morning full into my chest as I closed my eyes for as much as I dared while driving. Surprised, I caught the faintest hint of wisteria. I inhaled deeper this time, holding the fragrance so that it might imprint in me. That flower has obviously taken full advantage of the sultry night, leaving itself open to permit it's passion to drift on the infrequent moist night breeze. It was an intoxicating compliment to my tranquil trip.

I leaned my left arm on the car door, my elbow out the open window, and placed the heel of my hand under my chin. I was content, and my car knew the rest of the way. I found myself drifting back to the chain of events that brought me to Ameritherm, an induction heating company with about seventy-five employees.

One of my dental patients, Lou, worked there. He was very insistent that Ameritherm needed a massage therapist to come and work with the employees, and he was convinced I would be a good fit. There had been no other therapist at this somewhat conservative company. For in his estimation valid reasons, Lou felt *I* was the person to break the barrier and introduce them to massage. Being a sucker for grounds like that (especially early in my career), I said, "Bring it on."

In spite of being "just" a sales guy, Lou had some influence in the company: he was the unofficial-official moral-maintenance and employee-booster person. He was always arranging this crazy thing and that creative event to make people feel appreciated and valued at work, especially for the front office women whom he collectively called the Country Girls. He artfully presented his case to Dick, who was the founder and president and held the gavel for anything of importance to happen. Lou pulled whatever strings he needed to so that his concept became a reality, and a few weeks later, I had a debut scheduled. For this, I will be forever thankful.

I felt immense pressure and acute discontent driving this very route the first time. I had only been licensed for about eight months; I was still new. This would be the first time I would be working out of my element, the only familiar prop being my massage chair, which was folded up in the backseat. I had made all the arrangements by telephone, had never been to the company, had not met any of the people. The HR person Crystal had taken care of the scheduling. When I got there, I would be handed a list with twelve names, each with the amount of time that they had signed up for, either fifteen or thirty minutes. I would have ten minutes in between patients to change the face cradle and armrest cover and wipe my chair down. I imagined myself facing a swell of skeptical people, each with their own body language saying, "Go ahead, make my day."

I glanced down at the passenger seat beside me. There was my collective ace in the hole: twelve plastic-wrapped packages with six cookies in each. Three chocolate chip, three oatmeal raisin. I had been making cookies for my regular practice patients since I started working—a dozen of your choice after each massage—and they had become my mark. I saw no reason not to extend the convention to my new patients in Scottsville. These would calm even the most savage, skeptical beasts. Never underestimate the power of cookies.

I was making the slight bend into the town where the company was located practically on the sidewalk of Main Street. I still had my arm (and periodically, half of my face) out the window, trying to catch another sweet botanical scent to take with me into the building. I nodded to myself, recalling how hard my first day was. How difficult it was to work through clothing and how raw my hands were because of it. How I wondered just how I would survive the hours. How I shifted into self-preservation mode and, on leaving, made a very unconventional suggestion to Crystal that if I was invited back to the company, I could bring my massage table. Typically, this is not done in a corporate setting, but I saw no reason not to attempt it since I had use of a locking room with no windows. I could have people disrobe and expose their backs. Not only would they derive more benefit from skin-to-skin contact, I could be more effective than when I had clothing as a barrier to contend with. This would mean I could offer longer appointment times, say forty-five or sixty minutes. I did not mention that I would have an easier time of it as well.

I remembered a hopeful yet reserved smile crossing my face as I shook Crystal's hand; it was agreed that I would return in two weeks with my table, and the employees could then vote on which equipment they preferred. As much as they liked chair massage, they loved receiving treatment from the table. A few of the employees actually suggested that I never even think of bringing "that other thing" back.

So there I was again, like so many other Friday mornings, in the parking lot of Ameritherm, hoisting my portable massage table out of the backseat of my Taurus. With my basket of sheets and cache of cookies on the opposite hip, I headed in to set up for the six-hour treatment day ahead of me.

Sarah looked up from her desk as I came bumping in the door. A broad smile preceded her usual "Well hello, my darling!" Since I was introduced to Ameritherm, there have been four people who have taken care of my schedule; she is by far my favorite. Sarah is upbeat and personable. She is always willing to laugh and is especially genuine. She wears red shirts and very cool socks. In my clearly biased opinion, she is the perfect person to encounter when entering the company.

She was surprised to see me early. Schedule in hand, she followed me down the hall, explaining that she had not yet had the chance to clear the room for my table. "Sam is the first person on your schedule," she volunteered. "But I'm not sure if he is in yet."

I was routinely bending over unpacking my table, opening this, and adjusting that when the strangest thing came out of my mouth. "He's here," I stated with casual confidence while continuing to unpack. "I smell him."

I heard a short uncertain laugh behind me, then silence. I could feel Sarah staring at me while I moved around. I knew that it was not too often that she had nothing to say about anything. I turned to see an unsure look, like she didn't know if I was serious or if I was making an attempt at a barb. I explained, rather surprised myself, that I was quite earnest and that I did *in fact* catch his scent. I told her that was how I knew he was in the building. She opened her mouth. As she was just about to say something, Sam walked around the corner, ready for his massage. Sarah and I looked at each other in amazement.

Now I need to be clear on this. Sam does not have a body odor issue. On the contrary, he is quite clean. He is usually one of my first patients, and it is obvious by his sometimes-still-damp hair that he has just gotten out of the shower prior to going to work. It must also be understood that he does not use a strong soap or wear overpowering cologne or aftershave of any type. I reviewed all these facts in my head as I began to work on him. I came to the conclusion that Sam simply smelled . . . like Sam.

As mentioned earlier, I had a full day scheduled. A half-dozen hours to spend inside my head. As I worked, I found myself thinking about what had transpired moments ago. I was intrigued by the notion of detecting a presence before visual confirmation. It initially seemed like a new talent, though on closer examination, perhaps not. Suddenly, a flood of olfactory memories came pouring into my conscious space.

The pleasurable memories. The fragrance of the back of my grandmother's neck. How I could not inhale enough of the smell of my newborn baby's skin. Settling in at the end of the day to the sniff of sheets that had hung out in the sun and the breeze to dry. Catching the scent of my love many hours after we had been intimate. The wet redolence of the entrance of a deep cave. The instant comfort provided by the whiff of a campfire burning. The smell that tells me that I am finally home. Even the aroma of wisteria found this morning, still present somewhere in my nose. Interestingly, no one ever argued with me about detecting these scents.

Then the just-because-things-are-so memories. The rancidness of almost-curdled milk just before I went to drink it. The smell of my urine when it told me I was newly pregnant. The distinct odor coming from Shannon's nasal passages that told me she was developing a sinus infection. The mildewy insight that I had a small amount of undetected moisture somewhere in my basement. A preliminary diagnosis of toenail fungus when I had my face close to someone's foot. The time my nose detected a sparking wire behind an old switch plate. The hint in the air that a severe rainstorm was on the way. I recall being told it was not possible to distinguish such scents.

And then came the not-so-fond memories. The ones I just cannot seem to wash from myself. As a child, being forced to hug a greasy uncle, then having his stench on me for hours afterward because I was unable to immediately wash him off. The tang of a near-gangrenous foot. The time I knew my patient had lung cancer by the way the air smelled coming out of his chest. The smell of a room where a child was routinely abused. The time I knew by scent that my former fiancé had cheated on me. The way a person smells just before they die. I remember being informed that I could not have possibly smelled *these* things.

As I dismissed Sam, I thanked him for a very insightful session. I did not feel comfortable telling him that I smelled him before I saw him, but I did mention that he had given me quite a lot to think about. Because I usually share *some* but not *all* of what goes on in my head while I work, many of my patients have become accustomed to my cryptic postmassage mumblings. Sam just smiled and shrugged a "You're welcome."

As I prepared for my next patient, I expanded on all the previously mentioned memories and many more. At the time of each separate occurrence, these events initially seemed to hold little collective significance but, framed with the present context of my musings, were clearly pertinent. I was impressed and intrigued by the logical suggestions that the signs seemed to be pointing toward.

I was open to and excited about where my thoughts might be led. I worked to keep my mind clear and my breath present so that intuition might guide me. My cool hands started down Rick's cold back. Within moments, each was comfortably warm. I became conscious of something I always took for granted: the heat my hands generated. How, when the friction caused warmth, much more I could detect Rick's scent. I've often said that if I were blindfolded and I entered my massage room with any given patient on the table, I would be able to identify whom it was within a few minutes of touching them. I always made the assumption that this capacity would be due to my memory established through touch. I now realize that one of the hints I would have in the ability to identify a "mystery patient" would be the scent released and accentuated by the heat of my hands.

I smiled, thanking Rick for an insightful massage. I usually share more with Rick than many of my patients as he has always been very open-minded and receptive to entertaining alternative thought paths. I told him what I was thinking about as I worked on him. I told him I thought it was big. That it might even be in my book someday.

My next patient was one of the engineering people. I have learned that people come into my day (not to mention my life) in a certain succession for a specific reason. I took that person's place on the schedule as a sign to shift gears and approach this developing hypothesis from an analytical, factual perspective. It seemed to me a good time to revisit anatomy and physiology, the form and function of the sense of smell.

I'm not referring to returning to the first time I took anatomy and physiology twenty-three years ago for my degree in dental hygiene—when I was so caught up in dry memorization and comprehension of reams of information that I failed to grasp the real message. I'm more referencing the second time I took the coursework for my license to practice massage therapy. When I revisited these courses the subsequent time, I already had a solid understanding of the facts. I was able to spend my study time grasping and appreciating the complicated series of absolute and abundant miracles that make up the human body.

All smells start as chemicals in the air. They enter the nasal cavity and interface with the wet membranes deep in the nose. Specialized cells pick them up and send the information to the main interpreting areas located deep within the brain. The average person has twelve million of these receptor cells, which allow us to discern ten thousand scents. We can actually detect *one* single molecule of strawberry smell in a gaseous sea of *three trillion other molecules.* That is pretty damn impressive if you ask me.

Throughout the rest of the morning, the developing concept came together. Each person who signed up for massage on that special day, in their own way, helped crystallize my conclusions. Each person provided an opportunity for a new insight or realization. As it happened so many times before, my head had finally figured out what my body had always known and was inaudibly trying to tell me. I felt enlightened after completing that treatment day at Ameritherm. Enlightened, yet very disturbed.

Our sense of smell is not there simply to enjoy a pleasant fragrance, make us get hungry when we know the apple pie is ready to come out of the oven, or tell us when it is time to change the baby's diaper. Our sense of smell is used for things such as these, yes. But it is so much more than that. It is there to guide us. To instruct us, to inform us. To warn us, to prepare us. To protect us, to keep us well. To help us help others. To lend a hand in survival.

When humans were a much younger species, we were hunters and gatherers. Before we became "civilized," we relied heavily on our special senses to get us through any given day. Men were the hunters, where stealth and speed and exceptional eyesight ensured food for survival of their group. Women were gatherers; with their acute and well-trained sense of smell, they, in more subtle and enduring ways, also ensured the survival of those in their charge. Not just by finding the safest and best food, but to be alerted to developing health issues and to be sentient to changes that might compromise group safety or dynamics. At present, as the skillfully conducted and summarized study done by National Geographic Society indicates, women *still* have a better sense of smell than men do. I believe there is a reason for this.

Did you know that humans always sniff the air when entering a new space? That you take a whiff of something not only to just smell it, but to catalog, cross-reference, collate, then confirm it deep in your brain? Are you aware that your olfactory cells are constantly sampling the air around you for pertinent things to inform you of? It is true. Unfortunately, we are missing most, if not all, of the subtle scents our body is constantly sending us hints about.

In our society *today*, we are systematically eliminating our ability to sense what our body and other people's bodies are trying to tell us. A subdued scent can be completely obscured by a strong one. Yes, the molecules are there, but they are outnumbered. Most of the chemicals that the human body gives off (fixed, fired up, freely, or forced) are subtle. In an intimate space (defined here as approximately a five-foot perimeter) *without* other competing scents to obscure them, it takes awareness and concentration to be sensitive to their presence. In a space outside of an intimate contact perimeter, it is even more challenging, but not impossible, to detect them.

We have become obsessed with covering up natural, necessary scents. "Scent layering" has become commonplace. From stepping in the shower in the morning to getting dressed, a person can put on as many as twelve scented concoctions before leaving the house. That doesn't leave much room for our subtle bodies to communicate with ourselves or others. The water was a little less murky when we used simple animal-lard soap and water.

We have become fanatical with "fighting" or "eliminating" smells. Room deodorizers that plug in the wall. Carpet freshener. Diapers that are scented or that "lock in odors." All of these and more consist of harmful chemicals. If you can smell the product, the unnatural components are going into your body. If the smell is offensive, you are being told something. If something stinks in a room, air it out. If it is dirty, clean it. If the baby soiled the diaper, change it. Don't attempt to cover it up. Remember that the reason for the odor is that it hasn't gone anywhere. Eliminate the cause!

Isolation from each other is increasingly common. I fear this remoteness from other people is contributing to the demise of acuity of the sense of smell and our understanding of the very practical application. Because we are mammals, much of the chemicals our bodies release are actually produced more frequently and in greater quantities when we are involved in groups: families, friends, coworkers, passersby, gas station attendants, bakery people, and bank tellers. The relative constant presence of others keeps the pump primed.

A naturally occurring circle forms when children or adults get together to play or talk. Women friends face each other in conversation. A cohesive play develops during a football huddle. A number of students work together to solve a difficult problem. A family gathers to mourn. Collective human fear creates a mephitis that ensnares others. Sense of smell actually comes to play in *all* of these examples.

Is the sense of smell merely viewed as an appendix to modern life? Is this special sense important any longer, or has it become nonessential? Technology and modernization would lead you to believe much application of the sense of smell *seems* unnecessary. They are taking it away from us. No, wait. Allow me to correct myself. We are *allowing* technology and modernization to take it away from us. Practically asking "the Matrix" to strip it clean away. Allowing "progress" to stunt then seize from the human race something that I truly believe we still need, and now more than ever! Overly dramatic? I think not.

You know all those futuristic movies where advancement and technology are infused in everyday life, yet the beings are aware, intuitive, telepathic, in touch, and clairvoyant? If we don't wake up, that will *not* be us. Whether or not we even realize it before it happens, we will act surprised when it is gone. Many people actually go through days and days without interacting with a single human being, their awareness being denuded daily by lack of contact. If we don't use it, we *lose* it.

While working on my last patient that morning, I felt empowered and resolute. I made a conscious choice to develop my sense of smell. I decided to become an attentive student of the information suspended in the gaseous substrate constantly surrounding me, moving in and out of my body over seventeen thousand times a day. I promised to work hard to remove distracting smells around me: on my body, in my office, in my car, in my home. I became determined to use my sense of smell as if it was one of the most important tools I have to navigate with. I would begin to consult it. I would learn to rely on it. I would get to the point where I couldn't get along without it.

After packing the car, I eased my tired hull into the front seat, ready to gear down during the half-hour drive home. But first, I closed my eyes and inhaled deeply. I could smell the hard work delivered by my body. The apple I had sitting on the seat next to me. The possibilities provided by a new insight.

That massage day at Ameritherm turned out to be a formative, defining event in my life. It took some time, but I began to see the benefits of promises made to myself. I now notice things that I passed over before. My intuitions have sharpened and become more frequent. I know "things" before many others around me do. My life is richer, more contented. It is gratifying for my body to be using this navigational lead in the way intended.

The air around us is a rich sea of revealing scents. Clues we need to guide us are suspended and infused in this transparent ocean about us. Come on, dive in. Swim around. Immerse yourself in it. Take notice, and do not be distracted. See what you can learn, see what you can find. See what you can know.

Chapter Eleven

JUD

Jud did not like his body. He did not like his body, but he loved to golf. It may seem peculiar to place these two seemingly unrelated comments so close together, but through learning to accept one, he got better at the other.

When I met Jud, he was fifty-three years old. He refused to put much else on his health form. I got an address and one phone number out of him. He left most of the yes/no health questions unchecked. One of the only ones he completed was the last on my form, the "Do you have any other medical conditions I should know about?" question. He checked no. When I asked about his incomplete questionnaire, he said, "I already answered the last question. I do not think you should know about my health conditions."

On any other day, I would have thanked the person for their time and escorted them out the door. But not this day. I cocked my head and observed that he did in fact sign the waiver at the bottom. Something told me to proceed with this patient. "All right," I sighed for effect. "It has been a while since I flew blind. What the hell. It is your dime." He looked a little surprised but said nothing.

He also left the emergency contact line blank. I asked him if he did not wish to have a name here in the remote case that he would need acute care. He said, "Just let me die here. I would do the world a favor." He seemed to be having fun.

I looked over the rim of my glasses. "I can see that you may indeed be correct, but you would not be doing me one. I will strive to keep the world suffering with your presence." He permitted me to marginally enjoy myself as well.

I signed my portion of the form. I did not look up. "I need to inform you before I begin that the fee for your massage just went up ten bucks," I stated in an unemotional tone.

"What!" he said incredulously.

I put my hand up to halt his protest, then continued, "Apparently, you were so busy giving me a hard time you failed to read the posted signage." While I dated his form, I pointed to the area where my favorite signboard hung. One that I have had displayed in my massage room since the day I opened my practice but never had to actually put into *use* until that moment. It read quite largely in old-fashioned, nineteenth-hole lettering: "If you are grouchy, irritable or just plain mean there will be a ten-dollar charge for putting up with you." As he read it, I glanced up to watch him. When he turned his uncertain face back toward mine, my expression was stone-cold sober, but my eyes were smiling. I raised my right eyebrow. "Shall we start over?"

Things went better after that. Not great, but better. He actually let me in on a few of his health secrets. I got to the point where I thought I had enough information to cautiously proceed. I ran him through the drill for getting on the table. Before I left the room, he said the strangest thing. "By the way," he interjected, briefly stopping my exit, "I'm sorry you have to look at my ugly face for an hour." It was a plain offering.

"Your face isn't ugly, and I only have to look at it for the half hour that you are on your back." I pointed at the table and left the room to prepare to work.

I thought it rather peculiar that he apologized for how his face looked. As I washed my hands, I wondered what his issue was. I noted that my body felt calm—things would be all right. As I reached for the doorknob to go in, I had no clue how the session would go, but I knew it would never be put in the routine category.

The moment I undraped his back and began to work, more perplexing comments followed. "I bet you never saw a guy with no muscles," he spoke somberly.

"You have the same number of muscles as everyone else," I reminded him. As I moved to different parts of his stiff, nonfluid body, he had a caustic slam for each of them: he had a dumpy butt. He had the hairless chest of a twelve-year-old. He didn't know why he bothered to go to the gym because his arms would always be wimpy. He had legs like toothpicks. His hair was falling out. I was probably getting nauseous looking at him. He was sure it was skeeving me out to touch him. And so on and so on. Though I had a rebuttal for each insult, I finally got fed up.

I could feel a deep furrow form between my eyebrows. "You are offending me," I began very simply. "I will have to ask you to stop." I meant it. The way he continued to demean his form was upsetting me. He had an agreeable body. It was long and lean and proportioned well. Satisfactory muscle mass and no skeletal compromises. He was not too beefy and not to skinny. He seemed just right.

He said sorry but nothing else. I told him that I would stop immediately if he made one more destructive comment about the body I was working on and that from that point forward, any negative assessment was off-limits. "Pick something else to talk about," I concluded.

"Fine," he said.

So started his discussion of golf. He loved to golf. Loved the sport. The history. The tournaments. The courses. The professionals. The amateurs. When Jud was not doing something he was obligated to do, he was hitting a Titleist around. When golf season ended in New York, he would go south to play. When he could not get to a warm place, he spent his time at an indoor driving range preparing for the next season, which was, in his estimation, always too far away. I couldn't help but notice that when he was talking about his one true passion, his body softened and was much easier to work with and manipulate. Range of motion of his joints was greater, and they had a softer end feel. He no longer resisted me, verbally or otherwise. The furrow on my brow was replaced by a smile on my face.

Aside from coming to apparently make my professional life difficult, Jud sought help for low-back and leg pain. After I was finished, I told him that minimally two or three more visits would be necessary. That half-hour appointments would be sufficient to get the job done. That he would need to see a chiropractor in tandem with sessions at my office. Surprisingly, he was agreeable to setting up a schedule for both and still wanted to have a complete hour. He said that when I wasn't working on the parts that hurt, the rest felt nice; and if I didn't mind, he would like the longer appointment time. I said that it was fine, provided he did not breach the outlawed topic of conversation. We shook hands. "I don't have much of a handshake, do I?" he jested. I told him with a grin to get the heck out of my office.

The second visit went much better. Actually, it went great compared with the first one. From that point forward, the *only* topic of conversation in the massage room when Jud was there was—you guessed it—golf. This time, he shared with me how he got interested and how long he played and which courses he liked best. What his favorite clubs were, and why he hated slow play. While I worked, he chatted about reading the green and why "woods" are not made of wood and what makes a great caddy and why it was important to have a repeatable swing with the club. I told him I was impressed with the concept behind the naming of the Iron Byron. He was quite surprised to hear that I knew about the Iron Byron, a machine made to evaluate golf clubs. It is used to determine the maximum capability and performance of any club tested. (Byron Nelson was a pro golfer with a renowned *never*-deviating swing. No negative emotion or distraction would affect his performance. He was like a machine, hence the name.) The hour went fast, I learned a lot about golf, and Jud's body remained pliable so I could actually get my work done.

As I was preparing for Jud's third visit, I found myself wondering exactly what I would learn about golf that day. He was becoming a very cooperative patient who was shaping up to be quite easy to work with. Or so I thought. While he was on the table this time, he found himself talking about the problems he had while playing his favorite sport. I listened while he elaborated. He didn't always transfer weight easily from one leg to the other. He couldn't routinely keep his head down. Oftentimes, he would slice the ball. He felt the range of motion in his backswing should be much better. "My body just does not have the flexibility it needs for a complete backswing," he commented, quickly adding (so as not to piss me off) that he was not slamming his body—it was just that his body was not flexible enough to do what he thought it needed to do. He continued on with outlining the limitations of his body relative to golf and why he thought that if he had a different body, he would be a much better golfer. Interestingly, as the conversation progressed, his body was not as fluid and grew increasingly harder to work with. I was amazed at the implications.

I'm no fool. I knew that just because he stopped criticizing his body in front of me did not mean that he was still not feeling the need to do so. While in my room and under my care, he made a concerted effort not to express what he apparently thought to be truisms about his physical form. Though not spoken, they were still present. Jud had a long-standing negative body image that I was certain did not automatically go away in a matter of a few days just because I asked him to get rid of it. There was something significant here.

Jud seemed to have a fine body for golf. In addition to what I have already described about his physique, he had a high center of gravity (good for centripetal force, thus increasing clubhead speed!). An athletic build. Slim hips. A long neck. He appeared coordinated and agile. This seemed to me like the *perfect* body for golf. Intuition struck.

Rather than layup, I went for the difficult shot. I asked Jud if he ever thought about the fact that his negative body image could be responsible for his perceived lack of fluidity and flexibility while golfing. Perhaps his lack of self-love of his form prevented his body from moving at its full range of motion and in an optimum manner. Notice that I did not *ask* him if he thought he had a low self-image. My approach plainly indicated that I *knew* he did. He got mad. "You don't know anything about me," he chipped. I earned that; his response was about as abrupt as my assessment.

I continued to drive, "Perhaps not. I do, however, know a lot about your body."

I asked him to bear up and hear me out. I told him what I observed about his body. I shared with him what my hands told me. That he had a very fine body and that his disdain for it was most likely affecting how it performed for him. Did he ever make the connection between his perceived lack of flexibility and his negative body image? Could it just be entirely possible that if he liked his body, it would do a better job for him? Could it *just be feasible* that the dislike of his body was exactly what was causing the issue in the first place? He sighed heavily, "Go on." He gave the nod to continue.

I told Jud that in addition to the negativity he subjected his body to, I felt there was a strong connection between his suppression of appreciation for his form and his perceived deficit in function. Repression tethers joy and passion and energy. When he was expressing these emotions through his love of golf, his body felt looser and more fluid. The mind is so very capable of influencing and affecting the flow of the body. It can be the starting gate that holds back a race-ready Thoroughbred. Nothing can happen, no application can be performed until the go-ahead is given and the gate breaks open. When the mind sets the body free, it can execute virtually any command beautifully.

We talked about the fact that when someone is very good at what they do, either professionally or not, their body almost completely matches the physical requirements to fulfill and succeed at that passion. Look at one who dances beautifully or a proficient athlete. A surgeon. A construction worker. A painter. A potter. More often than not, the body that does the job is the kind of body needed to do the job in the first place.

I asked Jud to consider me as an example. The body in which I reside is so very suited for massage therapy, *and* I love to do it. I elaborated, explaining that the body I work with is low and solid and strong and flexible. It sports substantial shoulders, a high-volume chest cavity, and small thick nimble hands. This body has hips that are proportionately quite wide, cablelike spinal muscles, a compact core, and robust legs with thick calves. Granted, it is not the form of a model, but I could not think of a better body to practice the bull work of massage therapy with. "I guarantee," I told him, "this design is no accident."

Agreeably, the person who has the body suitable to pursue a vocation or pastime they love is a fortunate and happy one indeed. But which came first?

Does the type of body you are granted predispose you to a certain passion? Or does the passion you have hardwired into the future you somehow determine the type of body that one gets? This is not a trick question or a chicken-or-the-egg conundrum. I believe the answer is . . . both! You are in the body you are in for a reason. In most cases, and I mean *most cases*, the body in which your soul is planted is the one that is best suited to bring your spirit to its full potential in this lifetime. (There are a few exceptions, and this may seem quite unfair. All that means is that the plan of the Universe has determined that there is something else you are supposed to work on first. Your time will come. Count on it.)

He relaxed as I spoke, and I could tell he heard what I was saying to him. I was done talking. His muscles and body language told me that he was not mad anymore and that he was actually considering the possibilities. He was quiet. For a long time. "If this is all true, and I mean *if*," he began suddenly with qualified trepidation, "exactly what do you suggest I do?" I admitted that the possible solution was beyond the scope of my practice. I told Jud that I would give him the name of a competent psychotherapist who did work in such areas. That I thought he should schedule an appointment and talk to her about his body image and possible repercussions of it. She would be well suited to assist him further. "Now you are sending me to a headshrinker!" he said, feigning insult.

"Why not? Everything else works fine," I observed with a wink. "Seems your head is causing the problem."

I have noticed a mysterious and wonderful development in the process of my evolution. Many of the patients who have been sent to me are mirrors for my own instruction; each comes to me when *I* need a message to push me along on my path forward. Those times I have inquired or stated something based on intuition, it has in fact been my spirit, nudged by the Universe, addressing my ego. The wisdoms that come out of my mouth by way of inkling are words that *I actually need to hear myself*. In serious conversation, I have referred to this observable fact as the "template phenomenon."

In keeping with the apparent operating rules of the template phenomenon, universal energy in the form of words comes out of me and circles my room. It passes through (or around) my patient, then comes back to fall on my ears. Advice. Suggestions. Observations. Instruction that I engage my patients in. Basically, this is what I have learned: when I speak *on intuition,* I am either affirming something I am *already* doing, or something is being brought to my attention that I *need* to be doing. Especially with the latter, the message is always timely for my specific reality or situation. It almost seems irrelevant that my patients can also use this omnipotent guidance, yet as a vehicle, I am happy to oblige. I am very pleased to know that I do not suffer this usually painful process alone.

For the remainder of that day, it seemed that a putter was just a putter: I appeared to have escaped direct application of the Universe's trend for my unsolicited instruction. I didn't think much about Jud or the conversation that transpired as I wandered happily through the remaining hours. I was, however, insulating myself from impending reality. There was simply a time delay. A deferred hit was planned.

I was alone in bed that evening. My young women were asleep, and I could begin the process of shutting myself down. I closed my eyes and cleared my head. I released a relaxed sigh. Yet my contented feeling soon dissipated. I thought about Jud and my observation of his probable issue. I waxed somber. I began to think about *my* body image and how it affected *me*. Not in the public eye, mind you, where I am confident and self-assured and poised. I found myself wandering into my past physically intimate relationships. Where I historically had some stricture. It hit me, like many other salient messages, very hard. Very hard and dreadfully sobering and, up until the point that I reviewed the conversation with Jud, completely hidden to me. I had the heavy feeling it was to be a long night.

By now, you have a fairly accurate mental picture of the body that holds me. Allow me to provide a few more details to define the image. Add a slight rise and, at times, more than that, just below my navel. Go ahead, put a few faded stretch marks on my hips. Throw in some old-man hairs that singly grow where they do not belong. Imagine numerous scars from minor surgeries and trivial injuries. Include deformed baby toenails on each foot, and don't forget to include my ever-turning-platinum hair. There. Now you have a fairly accurate mental picture to proceed with. Certainly not a perfect specimen.

I always thought that I looked better in clothes. They would conceal the imperfections from my partners. The ruse would work, for a time. Inevitably, however, the anticipated time came when I would discard my garments. I want to make it clear that I would not *avoid* physical contact so as not to be seen naked. On the contrary, I easily moved to the bedroom. I would seek out physical contact because at the time, for me, it took the place of something that was missing in my life. Yet even unclothed, I still had my armor on.

The revelation came. It suddenly occurred to me that because of how I felt I needed to appear (or *not* to appear), I was systematically excluding myself from experiencing *complete* intimate pleasure. I manipulated my body in various ways to continue an illusion of how I thought others needed me to look. I would choose dim lighting or wait until dark. I would assume positioning that diverted attention from my "flaws." When I was on the bottom, even though I know my body really wanted my arms over my head, I would keep my arms tight to my side so my breasts would not fall toward my armpits. When I was on top, I would suck in my stomach. I would say I was cold so as to keep the covers over me when having sex in the light of day. I curtailed and suppressed the language my body wished to speak because of a hang-up *in my head.*

Though I was definitely enjoying myself, I did not allow complete unfettered fluidity, movement, or posturing. I knew this affected how I felt when I was engaged in sex. At times, it could be quite distracting and bordered on producing a nondynamic result. My preoccupation with the concerns took attention away from being completely present. I sat up in bed. Huh. Sounded just like Jud's situation, except with different equipment on a *very* private course.

I know how this happened. For as long as I can remember, the popular media of whatever-year-it-was consistently attempted to typify the "perfect body." Presently, the continuing trend has become raw and crass and way out of hand. It is now completely distasteful and offensive to me; but when I was very young, I fell for it, and it formed an anchor on me. The past and current parameters of "desirable flawlessness" are unrealistic and, for most of us regular people, completely unattainable. Yet instead of realizing that the ivory image is one that is just not meant for us and saying, "Sorry, I'm not going to fall for this crap," we look longingly at something we cannot have and secretly (or not so secretly) despise our own skin. It is like saying to the ultimate wisdom of the Universe, "You gave me something that I cannot use. I do not like it, and I want something else." This misgiving makes the body feel minimized and devalued, thus pulling back the reins on natural motion, shackling performance and function.

You cannot get another body. Learn to love the one you have. It is yours for a reason. Make it the best it can be, accept, then maximize the true gift that has been given to you.

And there I was—oh, impeccable timing of the Universe!—embarking on what would eventually turn out to be my steely, enduring final relationship. I had recently met a man in whom I was very interested. I felt promise and expectation like I never had before. I was wading into the warm frothy waters of sexual exploration. I hadn't really "been" with him intimately, but it was clear to both of us that the time was fast approaching: the air was thick with anticipation of it when we were together.

What if, I thought to myself, *just what if I proceeded into this imminent physical relationship with unfettered fluidity, passion-directed motion, unrestricted positioning, and unabashed comfort with my body? Sure, he would clearly see that I had imperfections, which, if we were together long enough, he most likely would discover anyway. But there could be a trade-off. Would I maximize my pleasure? Could I increase my enjoyment? Would it actually feel better than it ever had? Would his body also feel my unregulated passion?* I decided to take the risk. The easing that comes when a decision is made reached my body.

I made a promise to myself. When that opportunity came for us to finally consummate the building tension, I would proceed under the pretense that I was completely comfortable with my body. I would force myself to ignore the urge to bolster or divert or conceal. I thanked the Universe for looking after me and for sending Jud for me to listen to myself talk. I felt good. I slept well that night.

Soon afterward and as anticipated, my love and I came to be naked and alone. Though it was initially difficult, I did what I promised myself I would do. I always understood my hands held much love. What was not previously revealed was the presence of a deep undiscovered cistern of passion in this body. It was opened that day and brought to the surface. I continued to keep my promise to my body, and the benefits abounded. Perhaps it was meant to be—this untapped part of me was only to be released for him. To experience pleasure fully and completely. To, at long last, venerate my body so *it* could love what *I* loved.

Jud came for all his outlined visits. He briefly mentioned that he called the head doctor and that he liked her. He did not elaborate; I did not ask. We still talked about golf. He went to the chiropractor as directed. After the necessary succession of appointments at my office, his acute problem had completely resolved. He did not schedule any further appointments. He never came back.

One day, out of the rough, Jud called me. "I'm leaving you," he stated plainly. Apparently, he had great success with psychotherapy. He *was* playing golf much better. As a matter of fact, he happily shared with me that he was moving to Florida to go to a special school to become a golf pro. He also had aspirations to get a certification to manage a golf course. "Thank you," he said sincerely. "I have learned to take the negative emotion away from my body and out of my game. Because of that, I'm now having more fun and success than ever." He added cleverly, "I have become an Iron Byron!" I felt his smile through the phone. I smiled back. *So have I,* I thought, *so have I.*

Chapter Twelve

CHEVRON

Yesterday, I went grocery shopping for all of my bulk items. I hoisted the twenty-five-pound bag of granulated sugar onto my shoulder and started the short walk from the trunk of the car to the storage cabinet in the basement. As I lumbered down the stairs, I could feel the strain caused by the additional weight. I felt my anklebones adjusting to the added load. The muscles wrapping my knees tighten up. As I flopped the sack of sugar off my shoulder and strained to position it in the bottom of the cupboard, I was acutely aware of the burden the extra twenty-five pounds put on my body. I suddenly thought of Chevron. She still needed to lose over eight times the amount I just shelved.

I met her well over three years after starting my practice. Certainly beyond the realm of the rapid-fire messages from my hands that I received during the first two years of practicing massage therapy. When it seemed that I was being consistently, relentlessly, and unmercifully reparented by the Universe. I had evolved a little. Actually, a lot. Amazingly, when I thought I *must* be done learning, the Universe proved me wrong.

Shortly after I opened my practice, a newspaper article had been written about my new business. Chevron cut it out. She hung on to it. For a long time. Three years after began the many spaced-out, deliberate telephone calls to my practice inquiring about massage therapy. At first contact, she told me that she saw my article in the paper; and though she did not want to schedule an appointment at that time, she wanted to inquire about massage relative to therapeutic value. Chevron called a few weeks later and wanted to know which body parts I would work on and how I went about the whole process. A month after that came the call to ask how far she had to get undressed. I told her I would only undrape the area to be worked on, and if she was not comfortable with that, I would attempt to work within the parameters she would allow.

I thought we were close to scheduling an appointment. Yet again, Chevron thanked me very much for my help and said goodbye. For each call, I took the time to address her questions as I do not mind spreading the good word about viable treatment. After all, not everyone I speak with about massage becomes my patient.

By this time, I had recognized her voice when she said hello. She had a lovely intonation, and I imagined a petite young person when on the phone with her. "Hi, Chevron," I said cheerfully, "lay it on me!" certain she must have another question. She laughed. To my surprise, she wanted to know if I worked Saturdays. She actually wanted to make a half-hour appointment. I couldn't hide the surprise in my voice. "Really! I was not prepared for that," I joked. We got a session scheduled for three Saturdays out.

I hung up the phone. I wondered in the not-so-back of my mind why it had taken her so long to schedule an appointment. Obviously, she had not had bodywork done before, but that was the case with many of my patients prior to seeing me, and it did not take them three months of phone contact to make it happen. She could be just a very shy person who was attempting to feel me out to gauge the type of therapist I might be. Perchance she had some kind of birth defect or physical compromise that she was self-conscious about. Maybe she had a waffling complex. Perhaps she had touch issues or was not too comfortable with the thought of a stranger working on her body. I scoured my brain for all the possible scenarios so that I might play out treatment in my mind if any of the situations presented when she did in three weeks. Apparently, I missed one.

The morning approached, and I resolved myself to work with whatever issue she brought. When she got out of the car, all supposition and conjecture immediately dissipated. I wondered no more. I took one look at her and understood her issue. She was, quite plainly, the largest woman I had ever seen.

Please understand that I do not intend to be cruel or harsh. I am respectful of each and every package that harbors a soul. I have performed literally thousands of massages and have run across only one remotely close to a "perfect" body. It is irrelevant to me that all the rest are not. It matters not what someone looks like; it never has. I simply do not view physical presentation as a parameter to gauge quality of character or attraction. I hold no prejudices relative to presence of physical characteristics or lack thereof. But I do care about the *integrity* of the body. I love the human form. I hold it in absolute supreme regard. I respect all it does and am amazed by everything it is consistently capable of.

At first glimpse of Chevron, I kid you not, I grabbed the doorframe with my left hand and put my open right hand to my chest. An invisible weight pressed upon my shoulders, and my body became heavy. The space behind my knees ached, and my rib cage hurt. A grave feeling surrounded me, and my mood waxed somber. I simultaneously received the intuition that she was a victim of abuse.

I've always been sensitive to injurious treatment of the body, even as a child. While very young, I learned that my grandmother had been abused and mistreated. At the end of some days, she would sit at the Formica kitchen table with a stout glass filled with scotch and crushed ice, stirring the remedy around with her index finger before venturing little sips. I would come up behind her and smell her neck then rub her very large tired shoulders. Sometimes, she would tell of the horrors of her childhood. I would listen patiently and squeeze my knees together while she talked about her stepmother and the horrible things she forced my grandmother to do. I clenched my jaw and shunted the anger welling inside me to my little kneading hands. My grandma was a pure, beautiful soul. How could anyone do those things her?

When I was old enough to have my own library card, I would check out books on child abuse. I would walk into the house with a volume more fitting of a girl my age on top of the inappropriate ones so as not to arouse suspicion. I went up to my room and read the accounts and looked at the pictures. I would cry, and my body would ache for those babies. I felt fortunate that, though I was not happy with life as defined for me at that time, I was not one of those children. I wondered how anyone could do those things to a child.

As I got older, I began to read books about people who would self-mutilate. Girls who cut themselves or boys who would burn their arms with cigarettes. *National Geographic* always had detailed articles about remote tribes that would purposely scar or otherwise deform their bodies. There was never a lack of informative pieces on foot-binding or neck stretching or bizarre piercing customs or clans that would knock out front teeth with rudimentary chisels. Or the even stranger yet closer-to-home events like the guy who pulled a railroad car with ropes that ended in giant meat hooks penetrating through the skin of his back. I would be wide-eyed, and my heart would race. The back of my knees ached. How could this *possibly* be so? I did not cry anymore, but I would touch the page and sigh for the bodies that were subject to such cruelty.

As if this was not enough, I began to read and view accounts of torture. Sadly, there was no shortage of them in the daily news. Interrogation tactics.

Twisted treatment of kidnap victims. Retaliation crimes. Gang brutality. Detailed accounts of what had happened to victims of violent rape before they were killed. Each time I subjected myself to text and pictures, my body responded in much the same way as it always did, and I just could not fathom that these things could be so.

Repeated exposure to the incredulousness of the concept of harming a body, either someone else's or one's own, was leading me to a defiant end. Abruptly, I found myself done with my peculiar, morbidly curious focus. It was as if I was finally satisfied with my catalog of injustices. I had, at long last, sequestered enough awareness and anger to summon as a powerful force at some future time. I had successfully sensitized myself, and I began my mission. I took a private oath before the Universe. I vowed to some day and in some way be a champion of the mistreated and exploited and a tireless voice for the sanctity of the human body.

I attempted to shake off the unexpected flashback the visual preface of Chevron elicited. It was taking a while for her to get out of the car. I lost immediate conscious control of my body; my spirit moved to recognize another. Rather than stand and wait, with my arms open, I flowed off the steps to greet her. "I am glad to finally meet you!" I exclaimed with a broad smile in my voice and on my face. I reached as far around her as I could and gave her a giant hug. She immediately put her short arms over mine and held on. I felt their weight bear down on me. I pulled away just far enough to look eye to eye at her beautiful face. "I am so happy you made the decision to come," I said conclusively. I pulled my body into hers and hugged her again.

There we stood. In my driveway. One stranger eclipsed by the other. Unmoving except for a slight rocking side-to-side motion, the one that always seems to accompany a deep hug. Holding on because I couldn't even imagine why. We both took a deep breath at the same time. We were suspended in exhalation when the rumble of a passing dairy truck breached the moment. I broke away and asked if she would please come in.

She climbed the three steps with great effort. I looked at the size of her backside and found myself wishing I had the foresight to place a bigger chair in my massage room. She partially wedged herself into the seat, sitting mostly on the edge. Her cheeks were ruddy, and she was out of breath. She handed me the forms that I mailed to her in advance. I looked at the completed health history. Chevron was born over a decade after me. This surprised me. When I first saw her, I assumed she was my age. I suddenly thought of my slim youthful friend who oft chirped, "Television adds ten pounds, darling, and fat, ten years."

Chevron came to me for help with a complaint of chronic muscle tension in her back, neck, shoulders, hips, and knees. I continued scanning her form. Many boxes were checked yes. She had high blood pressure and elevated cholesterol. She reported cardiac problems. Circulatory compromises. Noninsulin-dependent diabetes. Swelling of her ankles. Shortness of breath. A tendency to bruise easily. Gastrointestinal irregularity. Depression. Difficulty sleeping all night. Gratefully, she was under the routine care of a doctor. Otherwise, I would have refused to treat her. I took a baseline blood pressure. It was high enough for me to ask Chevron for permission to phone her physician. I wanted to report her BP and confirm that her multiple preexisting conditions did not present contraindication for deep massage work. After some pointed treatment-specific questions from the triage nurse, I got the yellow light.

While I washed my hands in preparation for the massage, it occurred to me that I had never worked on such a physically compromised individual. Sure, I saw many patients with isolated concerns, even some with multiple considerations. But never one person with so many tandem chronic health problems. As I dried the water from my skin, I reminded myself that even before meeting Chevron, I committed to work with whatever issues she presented. I appealed to the Universe to guide my hands. I invoked intuition to direct me. I called upon my acquired knowledge to bolster me. I took a deep breath as I opened the door to go in.

Strangely, Chevron looked even larger lying down. When all of my other patients lie covered on my table, the edges of the linens drape the floor in delicate folds. The ends of the blanket covering her amorphous mass hovered far above the rug. As I undraped her back and placed my hands on her to begin, I thought about her tiny skeletal structure, probably no bigger than mine, encapsulated in thick gelatinous substrate. I closed my eyes and imagined a picture of what an x-ray of this scene might look like. It would appear as if her skeleton was levitating far off the table. I could not shake the heavy feeling at the back of my shoulders.

Chevron seemed nervous and initiated conversation that confirmed my suspicion. I made every attempt to keep chat light and nondirected. This proved to be difficult. Due to the increased height of her back on the table, I was massaging so far above my center of gravity that even if I stood on tippy toes, my strokes felt weak and ineffective. I was experiencing a great deal of trouble getting through the adipose tissue to the muscles that lay beneath and had to work to regulate my breathing, which changed due to the increased load on my movements. With great effort, I was able to get to some of the more superficial muscles of her back.

Fat tissue is very vascular. I was certain I broke numerous capillaries pushing through many inches of padding to properly manipulate the muscles underneath. The evidence of this would show up later. I found myself explaining to Chevron that she would most likely find some bruising in the days following her massage session. Suddenly, my moving body felt so very heavy.

The muscles I got to felt limp and flaccid, with little tonal integrity. Chevron reported muscle tension, but I did not detect this. I supposed that what she was actually feeling was fatigue on the muscle tendons and tiring ligaments that encompassed the joints of her skeleton. Though it is true that many of the physical structures of the body are unrelieved weight-bearing units, optimal function over time depends on a specific poundage-per-square-inch range. The over-three-hundred-pound load had far surpassed the physiologically precalibrated scale. A pulse throbbed behind my knees.

I had a lot of trouble adjusting to the fact that Chevron's breathing was labored while *not* exerting herself. Just lying on the table receiving massage, her cardiac and respiratory systems were stressed and operating poorly. After a couple of times asking her if she was OK, I stopped. I had to accept that this was her normal breathing pattern when she was not in a sitting position. There was pressure around my rib cage.

By the time I completed the half-hour massage, I was tired and sweaty. My body bounced back almost immediately from the session, but emotionally, I felt grave and exhausted. A pall of internal somberness grew inside me. My hands trembled as I washed them, and my mouth was dry. I stood at the sink. I cried.

I thought back to my initial intuition. I had no idea whether or not she was in fact mistreated as a child or if she had incurred some injustice later in life. I had no business asking; I realized that it did not even matter. However, my body was telling me I *had* witnessed abuse. For whatever reason, it was Chevron who was abusing herself by piling on the pounds. And make no mistake, abuse it was. Abuse of something that was given to her to revere and venerate.

Your body is not *yours*. Please don't immediately dismiss this comment as nonsense or, worse yet, get upset or overreact to what I just proposed. Open your heart. Hear me out. Contemplate what I have to say.

Your body is not *you*. You are your spirit, a timeless entity. You are you only as manifested in this lifetime. The body is simply the home your spirit is given to live in. To exist and travel in for this lifetime. It is an extremely competent form conceived to carry forth the essence of you. The body does not travel with you to wherever you go after death. Even if you don't believe your spirit goes anywhere, the body ceases to be. It is on loan from the Universe for as long as you are alive. The body you are advanced belongs to the miracle of the ages.

The relationship between the body and your spirit is intended to be a strongly symbiotic one: both to benefit, neither to harm. Your soul is provided a very nice place to hang out while you are visiting the earth this time. In return, the Universe expects that you will treat your physical form appropriately. You will care for it. Maintain it. Nourish it. Protect it. Love it. The well-cared-for body assists the young soul in development of conscience and awareness. It is a sensitive compass for use on the journey toward evolving your core. When this popularly named "mind-body connection" operates well, both companions enjoy optimal existence. When it does not, the results are catastrophic.

The body is a steadfast partner. Each egg and sperm harbor eons of encrypted evolutionary insight that animate when united. The body comes prepared with strategies to alert you when you are not upholding your end of the arrangement. The warnings are faint, the cautions whispered; it is a subtle yet persistent voice. When we as a species were more in touch with this quiet, unrelenting communication, we were better able to listen it. Tragically, we continue to move away from hearing range.

We all know that excess weight is unhealthy. We are all aware that obesity is rampant though I hesitate to agree with the popular monikers "epidemic" or "disease." It has been made painfully clear that Americans are the fattest people on earth. That our children are the heaviest of those of all nations. Science and medicine are only beginning to grasp the concept of just how significant the negative factor of added weight is on *every* body system. We may not all know that visceral fat, the adipose that forms around the organs deep in the body, is the most harmful of all. It actually mimics a gland and gives off toxic chemicals that are dangerous to all cells and tissues of the body. The inflammatory response that is triggered in the body causes widespread havoc.

Certainly, some amount of body fat is beneficial. It protects the body, keeps it warm. Provides an emergency food source and maintains healthy skin. It is necessary for ovulation to occur and lends a hand in many other metabolic processes. Every body on this earth has a predetermined range of body fat that is necessary for proper function and form. When the amount of fat begins to creep above the outer limit of that range, the subtle voice of the body begins to speak.

Allow me to interpret some messages the body sends, starting with that simple uncomfortable, distended feeling that comes when we simply have had too much food. Do this too often, we see cramping and bloating. Fatigue. Listlessness. Add the more serious signs as the weight piles on. Chronic digestive disorders. General feeling of unhappiness. Sleeplessness. Depression. Loss of libido. By the time the body is considered obese, it is virtually screaming for help. Chest constriction. Shortness of breath. Swelling of extremities. Stroke. Kidney failure. Diabetes. Certain cancers. A large percentage of somatic complaints and conditions can be attributed to excess weight.

We have so many scientific "early detection methods" such as blood values and vital statistics to help decipher the warning language from the body, but strangely have done little to end the cause of the problem, even when early signs present themselves. Easier to take a pill than change a behavior. We just mask the warning signs. Treat the symptom, not the cause. Continue to ignore what the body is working hard to tell us.

The evolution of the body's digestive course has not yet caught up with the present-day diet. Natural foods are complex and hearty and take time to break down. Energy is released slowly over a long period, a deliberate burn of sorts, like coals in a furnace. Many processed foods are simple and high in sugars and starches. The body converts them much faster to energy. A flash fire strikes, the inevitable cold void follows. Peaks and troughs in the fuel that is blood sugar confuse the body and stress critical related organs such as the pancreas. Energy that is not needed is converted to fat to be stored and hopefully used at another time. Unfortunately, all too often, this time never comes.

As a culture, we are collectively guilty of increasing idleness and indolence. The body was designed to move. To be active. To proceed through space and time with a surprisingly high level of movement and bustle.

Inactivity causes discontent in the body. The body sends a message of restlessness to the tenant inhabiting it. Because food is comfort, many times, we answer the dissatisfaction by eating. Yes, food *initially* makes us feel better, but an important communication from the body is misinterpreted and treated in exactly the direct opposite manner of how it should be. This endless cycle of feeling the body's message and responding with the wrong reaction increases the body's consistent yet louder statement of unrest. It is one of the root causes of how we gain weight. The body is not asking us to eat. It is telling us to get up and move about!

The body takes about twenty minutes after the first bite to register as "full." Within reason, it doesn't matter what we eat or how fast—it still takes about twenty minutes to get the signal. Given today's standard available diet, when the body registers "full," we have already eaten too much calorie-dense fodder. Portion sizes have increased dramatically since the 1950s, and the popular sentiment of "finishing everything on your plate" doesn't help. If we could just have the discipline to eat appropriate portion sizes (whether to satisfy true hunger or quell discontent), then walk away, in one-third of an hour, we would not feel "hungry" anymore. It's like magic. Try it!

Humans who live in remote natural areas with little change in indigenous diet do not get fat. The lack of overly available sugary foods, coupled with the complex, hearty nature of what *is* eaten, is a contributor to good body maintenance. Take into consideration that the person is reasonably active just to survive *and* is less distracted when the body talks to them. The combination of these four factors prevents excess fat from developing and taking over. The "civilized world" once had this dynamic working for it. We have lost much application of this ancient design, and the body is suffering. The cost of this sick, malevolent diversion from the intended design is principally, functionally, and monetarily higher than we realize.

The last ten minutes of Chevron's visit were intense. I returned to my massage room to see her sitting innocently with her arms draped formlessly on her heaving body mass. A picture of an impending animal slaughter flashed in my mind. I sat down to face her but said nothing.

She was actually quite intuitive herself. She asked, "This isn't going to solve my problem, is it?"

I said, "No, it really will not." She admitted that she knew most, if not all, of her issues were due to her weight. I told her what I knew about obesity and the body and encouraged her to work toward reducing the scale numbers. She said she was trying to lose pounds, but it was hard, and it was slow. I let her know I did *indeed* feel her pain. I held her hand, and I told her that I would be present for her to productively help comfort her body during the difficult time ahead. She thanked me for not making her feel like some kind of freak. She complimented me for treating her like a person, not a circus sideshow oddity.

That night, I lay in bed on my back in the dark, with my arms folded across my chest in a loving, comforting hold on this body. I knew what I knew, and I always knew it. But I never quite equated poor diet with mistreatment. Overeating with irresponsibility. Weight gain with disrespect. Getting fat with abuse. It forever changed my daily interaction with and reaction to the subtleties constantly whispered to me.

The retelling of Chevron is not meant as a pompous soapbox-style speech or an unsympathetic one-sided expression of hard-ass opinion from a perpetually skinny person. Neither is the case.

Primarily, I consider myself an anatomist and a physiologist. I exalt the body and understand how it is designed to work optimally and what it needs to do so.

Secondly, as I have already shared, my spirit resides in a five-foot-one, 128-pound body, which has been as heavy as 142. I have a long history of using food and alcohol as a palliative to my realities. Even recently, during some of my more anxious moments in writing this book, I have been guilty of using a bite of *this* or a drink of *that* to futilely offset my agitation.

The fact is that I know that I will continue to encounter daily struggle for balance relative to food and drink, but the message that Chevron brought to my hands has fortified me. The grip I *now* have on the situation is steadfast. I win the battle every day to push the "bounty" aside. I labor to protect the body the Universe gifted to shelter my spirit. I work daily to respect the body given to guide my soul.

Chapter Thirteen

BRYANT

On the bottom of my health form is a very definitive statement. It must be read and signed before I will treat a patient. It reads, "I understand that any illicit or sexually suggestive remarks, advances, or activities engaged in by me will result in immediate termination of the session and expulsion from this practice." It was on the basis of this clause that I found it necessary to release him.

The final letter he wrote to me stated, in part, that he took no inappropriate action before, during, or after any of our sessions. He concluded with, "When there is no trust in a working relationship, it cannot continue." Well, he was sure right about that one. In his letter, he lied and tried to hang the onus on me. What Bryant did not count on was that I *actually witnessed* his egregious act. I never imagined the trial of my "Do not test me" mantra would arrive in the context of such a long-term relationship. But then I suppose if it didn't happen with someone so close, it would not have been a real test.

I met Bryant through another professional endeavor. I knew him for a few years, and during the three or so annual times we worked together, I found that I genuinely enjoyed his company. Though he was significantly older than me (thirty-plus years), we had compatible souls, and conversation flowed freely while we worked together. He was well schooled and had a good command of many subjects and topics of interest. I liked him as a person and respected his experience and intellect.

Like many men of Bryant's age, he had served in the armed forces. His young married civilian life was interrupted when he joined the military and was called up after officers' training. He had been all over the world and seen many things. He had many experiences and spoke freely about all of them. He returned to the private sector when his tour was completed and worked until retirement in the engineering field at a major American company.

He could be difficult to manage. He was fastidious and precise. Exacting and efficient. He was regimented and had high expectations of those around him. Confident and brash with an almost-contrived gentlemanly wake. He was irreverent when appropriate and respectful when he needed to be. He was articulate and conversant, certainly not shy or bashful. He liked to dominate conversation and worked to maintain control of any engagement. He could be intimidating, and he liked it that way.

I witnessed his tendency to use this to his advantage. He felt the room became a better place when he walked in. He clearly loved himself, and he liked being who he was. One of the women who was working along with us approached me after he walked away. "He can be so difficult to interact with," she said as if it was completely necessary to share the observation. "How is it that *you* are so comfortable and familiar with him?"

"Because I can be," I stated simply. After a brief moment of thought, I added, "Because he lets me."

Bryant did not know I was going to school for massage therapy. He did not know I was scheduled to graduate that August and that, after sitting for my state boards in January, I anticipated having my license by February. As a matter of fact, I practiced massage for six months before the conversation ever even came up. When it did, he was all over it. I had heard him speak of his shoulder injury before, possibly incurred during the service. It was tight, and the range of motion was limited. He could not get it up above his head. Would I be comfortable taking a crack at it? It is not like me to back down from a challenge. I gave him my card and told him to phone for an appointment.

The massage therapy helped his shoulder pain and immobility. It only took a short period of time before he scheduled a one-hour appointment on a monthly basis. It was during these massage appointments that I got to know him much better. He did not wish for solitude as I worked. As a result, we talked about anything and everything. Our dialogue was engaging, and he gradually relaxed some of his social "military" ways. We had great conversations, and I assumed a mutual respect became inherent in all of our interactions.

After a couple of years of sharing, other tendencies loosened up as well. He began to divulge facts about his personal life. This is not an uncommon occurrence as any massage therapist (or health care provider, for that matter) will tell you. Though I would not condone many of the things people share with me, it is not my place to judge or condemn. I am obligated by the state to report confessions *of* or information *on* certain felonies, but otherwise take an oath of confidentiality. Through the years, I have learned that patients sometimes just need to tell *someone* something, and merely speaking of it *alone* relieves the burden that harboring the fact puts on the said person in the first place. However, many of the things Bryant shared went against my grain and precipitated lively diametrical conversation.

It has been said that you can take the man out of the military, but you cannot take the military out of the man. When I have heard this statement, it is usually offered as an *excuse* for retired servicemen who carried "bad habits" into their civilian life. I do not mean to malign members of the armed forces; I do think this sentiment applies to Bryant (and those like him) alone. His collective private behavior could have easily qualified as unbecoming of an officer. He was a heavy drinker and an incessant carouser. He took and gave orders well when he was on the clock, but when it came to his personal time, there was little discipline. He viewed alcohol and pleasurable female company as entitlement and justification for any job well done. He had a secret itinerary, one completely hidden from his wife and the rest of his life. Not the least of which included a woman or two on the side. He had preferences outside of "mainstream" intimacy. He slept with prostitutes while on tour and explored the sex industries of other countries. He did not see any reason why that should stop when he got back to the States. Suffice it to say he liked the satisfaction of doing his job well, then doing someone in whatever manner he felt like afterward.

After considering the aforementioned facts, you might wonder why I liked Bryant. Firstly, in spite of some of the more unsavory aspects of his personality and his unhealthy habitual tendencies, one could not take away his wit and sense of humor and intellect and capability. And besides, he reminded me of how I once was, though certainly on a less perverse, less grandiose scale. *I* came around. By the grace of the Universe through exposure to my patients, *I* saw the light. I watched how the process continued to work for me. I held out hope for him. If I could be enlightened, anyone could.

Secondly and on a less purist level, I *did* take great pleasure and satisfaction pointing out that the ironclad reasons for what he did were in fact indefensible. He had little viable rebuttal for my convincing and inarguable points relative to his behavior. There is nothing more emphatic than a convert vehemently discussing the results of their own hard-learned lessons.

In spite of his confessions, his behavior in my massage room was *technically* aboveboard. The few times I felt his dialogue was drifting into a realm I was not comfortable with, I called him back. He immediately .respected my request for decorum appropriate for my treatment room. I saw no problem with retaining him as a patient and as a friend.

There is one more thing you must know about Bryant. Periodically, when working in the base of his head during the completion phase of his massages, he would get an erection. You already know I view it as a physiologic response and are familiar with my standard line: "Don't touch it, don't move it, and it won't cause a problem for continuation of treatment." After the first time it happened, he asked if I was bothered by the occurrence. I told him I was neither impressed nor affected by it. I also took the opportunity to remind him of the segment of the release he signed a number of years ago, the one that specifically and *potentially* applied to this situation, should it get out of hand. "And remember," I cautioned, "*I* decide where that line is, not you." He assured me that he received what he called my "tactful warning" loud and clear and that he would not break the trust we had built into our professional relationship.

His arousal happened a few more times over the course of a six-month period. One day, before I began his session, he asked me to make sure I did not forget to give him his "five minutes of heaven." He was of course referring to his erection. I told him that if he ever called it that, or anything else for that matter, I would make damn sure it would never happen again. I was pissed, and he knew it.

The comment concerned me on a number of levels. Firstly, I got the impression through the request that he was now attaching a sexual connotation to a therapeutic venue. Given his history, I wouldn't put it past him. Secondly, had this become so important that it, in his mind, warranted verbal attention? Thirdly, why would he ask me not to forget a component of his massage (the neck and base of skull work) that I never forgot? Lastly and most critically, for the first time, I became concerned what he might do with himself *after* I left my treatment room.

I decided to be unrestrained about sharing my four concerns with him. I went down the list one point after the other without giving him a chance to speak. I told him I would be changing his treatment sequence and that I would not be working on the areas that seemed to stimulate him. He was welcome to refuse treatment, but my determination of how and where I worked was my prerogative.

By this point, I had known him for many years and enjoyed uncomplicated, uneventful therapy. I liked and trusted this man. Why was this happening now?

He decided to keep his scheduled appointment in spite of my removal of pertinent segments. I don't think he wanted to at that point, but he knew leaving would have been more incriminating than the stupid thing that came out of his mouth. He apologized almost too much and stated he did not know why he said that. I said that it hardly mattered—he did.

At times, my brazen directness surprises even me. I looked him straight in the eye and told him that I thought he was full of shit and that he was, in actuality, purposely testing the inviolability of our relationship. I told him that I felt he truly did not believe I meant to carry out indicated retribution for inappropriate acts and that the familiarity we enjoyed was being used to take advantage of me. I concluded by telling him that our friendship did not insulate him from the rules that applied to everyone else and that I was definitely not a pushover. "Do not test me again," I concluded curtly.

After a rough start to the session, things smoothed out. During the sessions following that visit, we were able to somewhat reestablish the calm waters present before the storm hit. I actually went back to working on his head and neck prior to completing his massage, and no "reaction" was elicited. It seemed we had both put it behind us. Unfortunately, I allowed myself to be lulled into a false sense of confidence. I should have acted more definitively on my earlier premonitions. I should have never given him another chance.

One morning, I awoke to a quiet unrest in my body. I was agitated, and the muscles that move my eyes felt overly active. My breathing was a nudge out of restful cadence. I wanted to move my legs. As I lay on my belly in bed, sipping my coffee, I began to decipher the message my body was sending me. Without a word from me, Michael asked me what was wrong. "I don't know," I said quietly. "Whatever it is, it's coming, and it's big."

I have learned well to rely on the wakenings in my body: the extraordinary prodromes it sends me. The gentle warnings I receive to help me prepare for whatever is to follow. I am not an exception to the human race. On the contrary, this forewarning system is hardwired into each of us. It tells us to be aware. To stand alert. To get ready.

Discussion of this inherent survival instinct sparks lively conversation. So many times, I have heard tell tales of feelings and hunches and intuitions prior to significant events in people's lives. Almost without exception, they will say something like, "I felt so strange that morning." Or "Something was just not right." And usually, "I couldn't put my finger on it." The story usually ends with, "I should have known it was going to happen!" Or "On some level, I must have sensed it was coming." Think about your own past intuitions. The presentiments are not imagined and are certainly not accidents, I can assure you.

My morning was frustrating. I was unfocused and out of my normal groove. I dropped my favorite coffee mug and chipped the rim. I burned my forearm getting cookies out of the oven. I sat down to write, and no words came. I was clearly distracted, waiting for whatever was to come. I decided to purge the corkboard in the hall next to the door to my massage room. It was a collection place for anything from expired coupons and old valentines to unnecessary business cards. It needed some attention, and organization usually provides some clarity for me.

My treatment room is actually a converted breezeway space. For those of you who are not familiar with this architectural gem, it is a room that connects a garage to a house. It has its own entrance door and is usually lined with numerous windows along each side. When they were built in the 1940s, they were not heated. They were used as "summer rooms" by the family, as well as a place to come in out of the weather and shed outer clothes and boots before going into the house. With the help of a start-up business loan, I converted the space into a year-round usable room. The floor and ceiling were replaced and insulated, pine paneling stripped and stained, heating and air-conditioning hooked up, electric updated, and the drafty old windows replaced with energy-efficient ones. Actually, the only thing that remained from the original breezeway was that door that led from the room into the house.

It was a thick wooden exterior door as it was originally built to be exposed to temperature extremes common on a breezeway. It had a small square face-height window with clear glass so that someone could look out from the hall onto the porch without actually opening the door. I was fond of the door because of its heft and deep wood grain, but the glass would certainly be an issue for the privacy of my future patients. I solved the problem by sponging a couple of coats of a soothing green paint on the inside of the glass. When viewed from the massage room, the effect was quite unique—it looked like frothy seafoam pressed by a thin sheet of ice. I was happy. My patients would have their isolation, and I could retain the beautiful door.

As I reached up to remove a three-month-old half-finished to-do list from the top of the corkboard, I knocked it off the single nail precariously securing it to the wall. It landed on my head, and the corner hit the window of my beautiful door. The impact caused a small scratch in the opaque paint job. "Shit!" I spat under my breath as I dropped some tacks in order to right the bulletin board. After I hung it back on the nail, I surveyed the damage to my window. I found that if I put my eye right up to the area where the paint was scraped off, I could see into the room. I opened the door to assess the surface my patients would see. Gratefully, from the treatment side of the door, the area of missing paint was virtually undetectable. As I picked up tacks, I made a mental note to paint over the scratch when I had an opportunity. It would not be today. I had patients coming in shortly.

One of those patients was Bryant. I struggled to put myself into treatment mode so that I could be present while I worked. I did wonder if my presentiments of early morn were in fact warning me about his appointment. But things proceeded uneventfully, no remarkable comments or dicey conversations occurred. The hour that comprised his appointment went on without incident. When I worked on his head and neck, he did become stimulated. I decided to end the massage at that point, and even though it was a nonevent, the presence of his arousal was abruptly unacceptable to me. As I finished out the massage with one hand on his chest and the other on the area of his liver, his abdominal pulse felt unusually strong. Suddenly, I felt alert and armored.

I started to leave the room in my usual manner, but not without locking my eyes on his first. My expression said, "Do not test me," but I said nothing. He shut his eyes as I passed him to leave. I closed the door behind me. Just as my hand broke contact with the doorknob, the skin on my scalp pricked, and I felt an invisible tug between my shoulder blades. I froze in stance. After a brief motionless moment, I slowly turned toward the window. I took a deep breath and exhaled deliberately and very slowly. My body knew what to do before I could dissuade it. I brought my face up to the window and closed one eye. I lined the open one up with the scratch of missing paint. I leaned forward.

I was appalled and aghast. There, directly in my line of vision, was exactly what I did not want to see. The linens had been pushed down to midthigh level. Bryant had his penis in his hand, and he was masturbating furiously. I immediately turned away, not wanting to watch while my room was violated. "That fucker!" I said under my breath as I rushed to the sink and washed my hands.

The cold water jolted me into collecting my wits. I needed to deal calmly with the situation at hand. I had little time and certainly did not want to give him any extra. I could not barge in and stop him. That would be a breach of reentry decorum: a health care provider must never reenter a treatment room unless they knock first and are granted permission to come back in. I certainly could not *tell* him I saw him do it. The room is supposed to be secure. I needed proof, and that was exactly what I decided to wait for.

After what I judged to be the typical amount of time I usually give a patient to get dressed, I summoned whatever strength I had to go back into my massage room and appear as if I did not just witness the most egregious act one could possibly take in the confines of my space. As I reached for the doorknob, a calm, frightening, deep anger smoldered inside me.

But on the surface, I knew it would be undetectable. Bob Marley sang, "Those who fight and run away live to fight another day." Though I was not running, I kept a calculated stance so I could get him out of my office without confrontation, *then* seek the proof I needed. I wanted him to leave thinking he got away with it. The impact of his irreversible dismissal after the *presumed* undetected breach of trust and policy would sting much more than an immediate challenge that he could easily deny.

Somehow, I was able to pull it off. He left without detecting my internal rage. As soon as he backed out of the driveway, I hurried back into my massage room. I gingerly picked up small corner pieces of the sheets until I found what I knew I would if I looked hard enough. "Son of a bitch!" I said loudly to no one in particular. I gathered up the tainted sheets and, holding them far away from my body, threw them in the garbage.

I sat down at my computer and hacked out a letter. I told him that it was my intuition that he had taken inappropriate action in my massage room. I stated that this was unfortunate and unacceptable. Bryant was informed that he would be given no more appointments and that no further communication with my office would be necessary. I placed a copy of the letter in his chart and drove directly to the post office to mail the original.

The events that transpired that day were discussed. Twice. Initially, I told Michael. That conversation was relatively simple. I told him what happened. I told him I excused the patient from my practice. I told Michael that if I saw Bryant in another setting, I would not entertain conversation of any type. Understandably, Michael was pissed and felt somewhat violated by association. But the issue had been swiftly and definitively dealt with. It was over. It was something to get past.

The second conversation concerning the gross breach of trust was much more animated and provocative. I met shortly afterward, as I did from time to time, with a group of massage therapists. We would gather every other month or so to offer support, discuss practice management and treatment modalities, and act as a sounding board for issues, problems, or concerns relative to our common profession. I had the floor and undivided attention as I told of the events as they transpired. Obviously, I did not identify the patient, but I left no *other* details out.

Pandemonium ensued. Everyone started talking at once. Some women actually got out of their seats. This is a hot topic for licensed massage therapists. There is a great, consistent effort by our larger professional body to separate and remove the insinuation of "sex for money" that has historically and unfortunately been associated with massage. It is common knowledge among licensed practitioners that disavowing breach of protocol elevates the practice. Allowing it drops integrity swiftly.

Various similar stories were retold by other members of the group. Some considered themselves fortunate that they had not had to deal with the experience. Things were winding down, and the room became quiet. One woman cried out to the silence, "Why do some people feel that they can do this?"

I heard my own voice respond to the question. It was a hauntingly similar answer to a parallel question I was asked some time ago. "Because they can." And then, "Because we let them."

Because we let them. The words echoed in my head all the way home. I had quickly recognized that the unplanned restatement of a comment made by me at another time was a critical marker. A challenge from the Universe. One I needed to reflect on. One I needed to pay strict attention to.

In hindsight, I should have let Bryant go long before he seriously breached the trust I thought we had developed. Though I do not sense he jerked off in my room before, he *was* guilty of incremental encroachment. I was culpable for allowing it. My body recognized it early. My ego refused to do something until it was too late.

We all have a bottom line. A point we will not go below. A boundary that we will not allow any to cross. This innate threshold, like the forewarnings we receive, is hardwired into us as human beings. It is a seed that is buried deep within us. We carry it with us into this world. It is a survival tool. It is a warning device. A husk to protect our consumable soul. But it does not develop completely on its own. Environment and nurture will either germinate it or stunt the maturity of it. Many times, the forces of growth fall somewhere in between. For example, if a child is taught through surroundings and rearing to listen to and value and rely on this system, it will develop successfully. If not, it won't. It is an entity that does not so much respond to *words* as it does to undercurrent and circumstance, situation and outcome. "Do as I say, not as I do" is a good illustration of what might negatively affect the maturation of this instinct.

For whatever reason (and it matters not), I did not have the nutrients available for my seed to develop completely. Because of conditions (or lack thereof) in my formative years, I did not learn to be protective of the innate steward of my soul. I realize that this is quite nonspecific. But suffice it to say for now that certain conditions were present. Others were missing.

Eleanor Roosevelt observed, "No one can make you feel inferior without your consent." I wish to offer an applicable modification to that quote: no one can take a piece of you without your consent. Because that is *exactly* what happens when you allow someone to disrespect your line of individual integrity. *Allowing* a breach of your boundaries extracts a part of your soul. Acts of birth and unmitigated violence notwithstanding, adults have *complete control* of whom they allow or do not allow to "off" a piece of themselves. Some may disagree. That is OK. For I will debate this all day long. Remember, I have been there. For too long did I reside in a flooded, stagnant field.

I oft traded and squandered my option to resist in order to gain what seemed to be, at the time, an immediate advantage. Yet when viewed at the end of a deprived growing season, they were poor choices at best. Each time I allowed someone to step past my line in the dirt, I lost a little of myself. By the time I acclimated to my adjusted-then-readjusted standards, I had to fight so hard to advance. I had to summon so much energy to protect my retracted front line. The enemy had gotten deep into my sacred territory. I had to battle fiercely to get them out. And myself back.

The older one gets, the further along on the chosen path one travels and the less of oneself there is left to continue on the journey. Strangely, earning my license to practice dental hygiene turned me back toward the fork to the higher road. For whatever reason, professional integrity moved me. It *mattered* to me. I now had a higher power to answer to. I took an oath. I was to help and do no harm. My actions and behavior would be subject to monitoring, and I would be held accountable.

Having babies pushed me even further along the right path. Being responsible for the successful development of two little beings was a duty I took rather seriously. No other force motivated me to strive to adhere to my principles as much as the mantle of becoming a mother. We are getting along better now, but early on in my divorce, in a moment of anger, my ex told me if the girls turned out to be screwed-up adults, it would all be my fault. I told him there was no doubt there, but if they turned out to be wonderful women, I would *also* accept all the credit.

It is hard to extract oneself from a bankruptcy. Yet every good fight won reinvests in the sources necessary to get and keep things healthy. Fortunately, I read the signs and allowed myself to be placed in a nutritive environment. The final buttress on the garden wall I rebuilt was my formation and subsequent practice as a massage therapist. I was completely accountable. I was ultimately responsible. I alone would make it or break it. This empowering position coupled by the numerous sanctioned lessons I had been force-fed along the way catapulted me forward.

My strength swelled through somber recognition of numerous events of acquiescence. I grew straight and sturdy with each mounting adherence to my encrypted code. Rediscovery of the healing power of standing up for one's principles pushed me into perpetual bloom.

One day recently, during a heated discussion, an exasperated Michael rhetorically tossed a question my way. "Why is it that you are so goddamned principled?" he asked, offering a conceding end to a dicey discussion. I have been on the other side. It wasn't pretty. I would never go back. I smiled at him and then at myself.

"Because I can," I responded defiantly. Then I softened, "Because I let myself."

Chapter Fourteen

ONE TO WHOM I GIVE NO NAME

Evil does not force it's way into our lives. Negative energy does not pry open our souls. Malevolence does not rain uncontrollably upon us. The devil does not wedge his foot in the door. We make it easy. We smile. We welcome him. We let him in.

I met the one to whom I give no name at a time when my practice was solid. Many of my patients, the ones I have written about and most of those whom I have not, helped define the composition of where I was and what I did. I was solid and rooted in only having those people I wanted in my life. I enjoyed the liberation of practicing massage therapy within relationships that were life-giving, authentic, and mutually reverent. My definition of success, I would often tell people.

I was also strong and unyielding. I was, at long last, in a truly committed relationship. I was done looking; Michael was the last man standing. I had found my partner for life and cast off those constraints that kept me a prisoner of myself. My resolve in keeping this final relationship intact was unrelenting and impenetrable.

While at the gym one morning, I happened upon the one to whom I give no name, working on a machine on the opposite side of the circuit from me. About midfiftyish. Well-groomed. Not unattractive. We made eye contact, I nodded, he winced. "My back," he said factually. "I've really been struggling with it."

Being me, being helpful, being a massage therapist, I, of course, jumped in. But not before a brief, almost imperceptible, hesitation. Within split seconds, I subdued the prodrome. At the time, I didn't understand it, so I dismissed it and went on. It would later prove to be something I should have heeded.

Through conversation about his injury and my profession, I found him to be quite bright and articulate. I asked if he had tried massage therapy—it couldn't hurt, and it could only help. After I finished working out, I gave him my card as he had asked. I shook his hand. He seemed genuinely surprised by the firmness of my grip and said so. Polite. Made eye contact. Cordial.

To my surprise, he phoned that afternoon for an appointment. He scheduled a half-hour treatment slot. He arrived a week later in a polished luxury car. In spite of the fact that it was a cold mid-January day, he had with him a little yipping dog that was jumping around in the backseat. He was on time. In impeccable casual dress. As he approached the threshold of my office, he told me he liked my toe ring. I could feel my right eye close ever so much and my head tilt a little to the same side. The combination of these gestures usually means "what the hell does that have to do with anything?"

Health history was completed, the usual instruction about positioning was recited as it was hundreds of times before, with no deviation whatsoever from my rhetoric. He looked around my room. "I'm enjoying learning about your space," he commented. "It tells me a lot about you." I found myself being somewhat annoyed at this comment. Usually, an observation such as that would not even faze me. I would thank the person and move on. But I said nothing. Uneasiness was growing. Deep in the center of my body, my warning sensors were going off.

I left the room to let him follow my instructions for getting on the table. I washed my hands and prepared myself for work, allowing enough time for him to disrobe. I knocked on the door and asked if he was ready for me to come in. "Yes," came his plain response. My reticence cautioned me. I started to open the door and hesitated, then peered through the crack into my room. I could see that he had disrobed, but was lying directly on top of the sheets, completely undressed. I quietly closed the door again and stated in a short firm voice that before I would enter the room, he needed to be *under* the sheets.

This had happened once before with a dentist I worked with: he had never had a massage. At the first visit, I believe that he was sincerely confused and very nervous. He did not drape himself. I have since then greeted him with a smile as Dr. Butt-naked. We got past it and went on to establish a comfortable routine therapist-patient relationship. But this was different. It took on the likings of a game. Of a test. Of me. I felt myself becoming battle ready.

He responded immediately; I could hear him get under the sheets. I asked him again if he was indeed under the sheets. "Yes," came the response from the other side of the door. I entered to find him to be positioned properly under the linens and draped.

"Don't ever do that again," I commanded curtly.

"I'm sorry," he offered. "I guess in the confusion I misunderstood. I myself thought it a bit strange that I should not be covered." I gauged his response. I told him the next time he was unsure of instructions, he should ask for clarification. *This guy is so full of crap*, I thought to myself. But I like to give people the benefit of the doubt. There have been many patients with whom things had started out rocky and ended up glasslike.

I initiated the session. As I started on his back, he attempted to make light conversation. He asked me to tell him about myself. I chose an informational topic. I told him about my practice. I chose a critical tidbit topic. I let him know that I had an amazing partner named Michael and that I was content and secure in my relationship. I chose a safe topic. I told him I was working on a book. That it was in the midstream stages. That it was set in the context of my professional experiences as a massage therapist, but that it really addressed my own deliverance. He asked me if I could give him specifics. I told him no.

"I'm writing a book as well," he said. I was happy to have the conversation shift and felt some strange fellowship with another struggling author. I asked about the content of the work. "It's about why men lie," he explained.

"Really!" I said. "We have needed a definitive work on this topic for some time now," I said agreeably. "Now *that* is a book I would definitely read." Things were going smoother now, and I was almost completely at ease. Almost.

Usually, for a half-hour acute-need appointment for lumbar pain, I allot twenty minutes for decompression of the related muscles of the back. I then position the patient on their back and spend the remaining ten sitting at their head, manipulating the neck and shoulders. During a moment of idling conversation while working on his back, I had a strong intuition, hearing that voice say, "Don't roll him over. Keep him facedown." I dismissed this at first, but through the course of working, I *again* heard the message in my head. After the third time, I thought, *All right, I get it!* in response to the invisible prodding. I literally shrugged my shoulders and nodded to the Universe. I would honor the strange command and alter my usual treatment method. I did not understand it, but I thought it best to defer to the wisdom of that which is larger than me.

The usual wrap-up and dismissal went without incident. I waited until the car pulled out of the driveway and turned to reenter my treatment room. I felt strangely ungrounded as I reviewed the events of the last forty minutes or so and then chalked up my agitation to the butt-naked happening. It seemed as if I was trying to convince myself.

Typically, I will solve most concerns on my own. I will take private time to work through my issues to arrive at a plan of proceeding, and I do not often ask for assistance in matters of interpersonal dynamics. However, these circumstances were quite another matter, and preserving the cohesiveness of my relationship with Michael came to mind. After short consideration, I made the decision to break from my solitary approach.

When Michael got home from work, I told him about this patient. I relayed all the events as they occurred and my feelings when they did. The fact that I was talking about it meant that I was concerned. The fact that I was concerned caused him to become so.

"Are you going to treat him again?" he asked, hoping I would say no.

"Well," I responded, "he didn't schedule another appointment, and I am certainly not going to ask him to."

Michael's brow was furrowed. He told me that if I had no objection, he was going to ask around at the gym to see what was up with this guy. Michael had been a member for many years and knew just about all the staff and early-morning workout people. I kissed him and told him to get back to me with the reconnaissance report.

I saw the one to whom I give no name at the club a few more times. He stated that his back was feeling better, and along with a few adjustments from the chiropractor, he was doing well. Though he did not ask to schedule another appointment, and he did not say he would call for one, I began to get the sense that he was hovering around me. He would seek out small conversations each time I would "run into him."

He was flushing me out. Assessing my caliber. Engaging me to learn about me. Initially, I found myself being almost unfriendly at his presence. I had to work at being cordial. But as time went on, I viewed the conversations as civilized challenges. Soon I began to see interactions with him as a battle of stealth and strength and wits. Nobody puts *me* in the place where I do not have the upper hand. *I* do not back down. I decided that I was going to get in it. I put my war paint on.

The circling face-off began. My reticence turned to subterfuge. My avoidance became confrontation. My distancing changed to active engagement. A few have told me that some of my most impressive characteristics come out when I am pushed. I can judiciously apply witty sarcasm, with fearless posturing and caustic humor. I must confess to loving being in this place. I regularly suppress and withhold my battle-driven soul, but when I unsheathe *this* sword, a dormant part of me comes alive.

Without warning, he called for another appointment. He asked if he could schedule an hour. I told him that thirty minutes would be sufficient. *Things will be different this time,* I postulated. When he pulled in the driveway, I saw that poor little dog in the backseat again. On many occasions, I had seen the tiny pet in the car at the gym, out in the cold, yelping to passersby. "That dog is a prisoner," I said out loud to the snow. "Why do you keep that dog in the car all the time?" I more observed than asked when he approached my office door.

"She likes being with me wherever I go," he responded.

"Doesn't *look* much like she does," I stated flatly.

For this second visit, I postured myself as the ultraprofessional, the Ice Queen, as my friend Bev referred to this role I sometimes must play in order to maintain direction and control in my massage room. "This time," I told him after a brief inquiry as to the status of his lumbar pain, "get *under* the sheets or else . . ."

He put his hand up apologetically. "I know, I know. I will be out of here. I don't make the same mistake twice," he concluded. Satisfied, I left the room and returned to find him and everything else in perfect order.

Though the rest of the visit went without notable incident, I was making mental notes and gathering information for myself while I worked. He had a definite strategy of casually trying to find out as much about me as he could. Not to make conversation, but to learn. To ascertain. I turned all initiations back to him so my personal life was not the central focus of the conversation. He responded only as if he was playing along.

I made the decision based on my intuitions from the last visit not to turn him over. I kept him facedown. Things were going well. I was driving. Suddenly, just as I began to feel myself relax, I felt this incredible rush of energy from my body. Not the one I give freely to my patients or my children or my lover. But one that was taken from me, like my fortress was forced open, and all my warmth escaped into a cold lifeless void. I felt the drain of life from my body against my conscious will, like there was a struggle initiated for my personal space.

I immediately put up an energy wall in my chest and stopped the vigorous draw of my breath into his body. My hands continued to move in a robotic fashion, yet I completely disconnected myself from him. I intently sniffed the air for additional inferences. His pulse, respiration, and breathing did not change at all, but my heart was racing. By this time, the last few minutes couldn't pass fast enough, so I decided to end the massage early. Something wasn't right, and I didn't like it.

When I dismissed him, I told him I was done. He said that he could see that. I said, no, I was *really* done. I indicated that I could not help him, and I would not reappoint him for any more visits. He looked rather surprised but did not ask what the issue was. I did not offer an explanation. He paid my fee and then went back into his wallet for a tip. As he pulled five dollars out of his billfold, I told him with a self-assured smile that I earned my fee, but I did not want anything more from him other than to get the hell out of my office.

I phoned my fighting partner afterward. I told him what had happened. Michael listened patiently for me to finish. Then it was his turn. He told me that just that morning, he had managed to get some info on this guy. That he was relatively new at the gym. That he was causing some trouble, and some of the female members had complained. That he was hitting on one of the young personal trainers he hired and was making her increasingly uncomfortable. She decided to drop him as a client after he told her she reminded him of Julia Roberts in *Pretty Woman*. That he was dating one of the receptionists at the check-in area. Michael told me her name, and I knew whom it was, a petite submissively postured woman. "I asked her if she knew anything about him," Michael continued. "And she denied even knowing him!" he said emphatically. "This guy is a predator, Mare," he added as if it was not already understood. I suddenly remembered the yipping dog that traveled enslaved, and I was immediately afraid for the front-desk woman.

When Michael came home that day, he hugged me hard. I told my love that I went from being concerned to being angry that a person like that stalks the earth. I told Michael that though I dismissed him from my practice, I wasn't done yet. "I'm gonna take him down," I whispered into his ear. Michael pulled away and grew visibly upset. He told me that he preferred that I not mess around and that this was not a game and that it might be best if I just left the whole thing alone. "This guy is a menace," I charged. "He is preying on women." I was going to do everything in my power to stop it. "I will not be guilty of inaction!" I finished defiantly. Michael sighed despondently. He said that my pride and stubbornness were getting in the way of my usually clear vision. I told him I would be fine. Unwisely, I ignored his plea.

On the way into the gym the next morning, I scanned the parking lot for my nemesis and his captive pet. No sight of him. After my swim, I decided to go get a bagel before I went on my way. I walked into the deli, and *there* was the one to whom I give no name, sitting in a sunny spot at the window, reading the paper. We made eye contact, and I nodded. As I walked past him, without looking up from his paper, he suggested I join him after I got my order. *I'll show him!* I said to myself as I waited for my bagel. *I will not run. I will not hide. I will face him.* I thanked the young man at the counter and stepped toward the table. Every bone in my body told me to keep on walking. But no. I sat down.

"We have gotten off to a bad start," he began. I said nothing. "I am going to come clean," he said. *Like that is possible,* I thought. I chewed my bagel and still said nothing. "I find you very attractive. You are very smart. Extremely witty. Your confidence is inspiring." He went on to tell me that in his wallet he carried a slip of paper. On it were four adjectives that described what he needed for a perfect partner and a perfect relationship. I asked what they were. He told me. He added that when he met the woman who fulfilled this description, he would know that he met the person meant for him. "You fit my requirements."

I sat back in my chair in astonishment. "What a pompous ass," I said way under my breath. I reminded him that I was very happy and content with my relationship. I asked him what he thought his girlfriend at the gym would think about his finally finding the woman "worthy" of his company. He was taken aback by this supposedly hushed fact. I told him that I had no interest in him and no desire to speak to him anymore. As I got up from the table, I remarked coyly, "I noticed that the word 'love' is not on your pathetic list." I left my garbage for him to clean up.

A couple of days later, I received a small card in the mail. On the front was a poem by David Whyte from *Where Many Rivers Meet.* One of the passages from the poem read, "In this high place it is as simple as this, leave every thing you know behind."

"Holy shit," I said to myself. My hands were shaking as I opened the card. The handwritten inscription read,

Mary Beth,

Thank you for our conversation this morning. I was moved and inspired and find myself embraced in the joy of what we are creating. If "we" stopped today I would know that I was known finally, and that would fill a very important hole in my life. Someday, I hope to give all of this heartfelt (more like pounding!) love, passion and commitment that I have welled up while I have been waiting for her to knock at my door. I hope you come in . . .

Well, this about completely freaked me out. I was angry. I was concerned. This guy just didn't listen. I was a little scared. What had I done? I sat on the couch. The realization hit me that I made this all possible. This guy had played to my weaknesses—which I saw as strengths—to continue to engage me, and he almost succeeded in I didn't even want to think about what. I was blinded by pride and bravado. By this point in my development, I had certainly learned a lot. Many things, clearly not everything. I finally comprehended that I might actually be in a dangerous place.

Since the situation had already caused some low-grade conflict between Michael and me, I wondered whether to call. I hate I-told-you-so reckonings. Yet it occurred to me that by not calling, I would be allowing the one to whom I give no name to put a chasm into our cohesive, honest relationship. It was time to suck it up. I dialed the phone.

"I want him out of our lives NOW!" was Michael's not-so-calm response. Understand that Michael never *tells* me to do anything. He may ask of me. He may request consideration of me. He may suggest. He is astute, and his understanding of how to "deal" with me is complete. He knows that the surest way to compel me *not* to do something is to tell me I *have* to do it. Though given the situation, I felt his response was an appropriate call for an overdue definitive action.

Michael decided to get involved. I did not discourage. Michael usually is gone from the gym before I get there, so he spread the word around before I arrived. He informed one of the very large trainers that I was having real trouble with this member and asked if he would watch out for me. News spread fast that morning. Apparently, the one to whom I give no name alienated quite a few people, men and women alike. By the time I arrived, the air was thick with anticipation. Many nodded knowingly to me as I walked through the weight area. A few of Michael's friends positioned themselves on equipment in close proximity to where I was working on the low-back machine. The gigantic trainer leaned against the wall, with bulging arms folded across his massive chest, watching.

As if on an unaware cue, the one to whom I give no name entered the gym and unknowingly began to walk the gauntlet. He pleasantly greeted a few members but got no replies, no smiles, just frigid looks. I watched him becoming increasingly uncomfortable as he wandered into the unresponsive cold air of combined distrust. He quickly surmised that something was amiss and figured out *he* was the focus of the unwelcoming reception.

He self-consciously walked toward me, quickening his pace. Desperately hoping that there was a least one friendly face in the hostile environment, he stopped directly in front of the machine I was working on. I came at that moment to upright position on the apparatus, eye level with him. Right before my now instantly *opened* eyes, I witnessed the most hideous thing I have ever seen.

His face somehow subtly morphed into an ugly dark caricature, like when two left sides of a person's face are put together to form one expression. His skin turned ashen, and gray shadows formed above his cheekbones. I froze, and my eyes widened as they fixed on his mouth. His lips were forming words, but I heard nothing. I was deafened by the shock of seeing an inky mist vaporizing out of his orifice as he formed his silent words. I backed away to see a repulsive black aura come about his head. The Universe had let me see that I was in the company of one of the blackest hearts walking this part of the earth. His exact plan to get it was hidden, but he wanted my soul.

I locked my eyes on his as I slowly got off the equipment. "I know what you are," I hissed. As I slowly walked away, I caught a glimpse of the big trainer and my other sentinels moving toward him. I never found out what transpired after that, and I didn't care.

When I got out of the workout area, my paced quickened to the front desk. There was the petite victim of the demon. I told her I needed to speak to the director immediately. She asked what it was concerning. *Who knows what he has told her about me,* I thought to myself. I told her it was none of her business and to just get him. I spent a few moments informing the owner as to what was skulking and prowling around his facility. I told him that his staff and members should not have to endure this behavior and that I thought it was prudent to exile him. If he did not take the indicated measure, I would take further action.

I got in the shower, my chest heaving as the cool water ran over me. I wanted to wash him away forever. I needed to be home fast—there was one more thing I needed to do. Twelve miles later, I made my last contact with him. I called his number; he answered the phone. Apparently, his gym visit had been cut short.

"Hi!" he sang, obviously pleased to hear my voice. He *still* didn't get it! I told him never to approach me or call me or talk to me again. If he did, the police would be contacted. "Just like that?" he asked. "I don't even get a reason?"

"No," I stated definitively and hung up the phone.

On Monday morning, I showed up to exercise. In the weight area, the same group of people were there as the day of confrontation; but the mood was light, almost celebratory. Michael's friend gave me a high five as he walked by. The big trainer formed "guns" with his thick fingers and beamed. When I walked into the locker room, the pretty personal trainer stopped me and grabbed my arm. "Thank you," she smiled, "he's gone." As I was leaving, I passed the front desk. I stopped and turned to inquire as to the whereabouts of the girlfriend of the demon. The receptionist informed me that she quit suddenly last Friday. I heard his voice in my head, saying again, "She likes being with me wherever I go."

This chain of events that occurred at my hand made quite an impression on me on a number of levels. Primarily, my body knows I am in danger long before I do. I was so very foolish to ignore it. I would *never* disregard it again.

Secondly, I learned to continue to keep what I treasure close. When facing the consequences of my recklessness, I discarded isolation and deferred to the power of inclusion and the subsequent strength of two. Telling my partner of my self-created problem not only assisted in the solution, but also strengthened my resolve to keep the relationship solid.

Most importantly, I *finally* learned the importance of disengaging my ego. Not only when it is evident that it will harm, but also when the consequences may not be so obvious. My unhealthy sense of self was the last anchor to fall from me. The liberation that I have experienced due to this exfoliation is like no other freedom I have earned.

As we lay in flannel that night, I told Michael I was pleased that the one to whom I gave no name was out of our lives. Yet I couldn't help but think about his captives and the disquieting fact that he would most likely hunt again somewhere else. Michael was equally moved as I. A short time later, he wrote a poem to chronicle the battle and to honor the outcome. I would like to share it with you. Of all he has written, it is by far my favorite.

The Predator

Scrutiny from a distance
To consider my approach
An unsuspecting quarry
A probable new host

This latest prey is special
Distinctive posture, self-assured
A different slant must be taken
Her instincts must be blurred

An appeal to the intellect
A challenge of the mind
Weighty banter will provoke
And stimulate this kind

I'll test this young soul's metal
My scheme will now unfold
Wanton failure I shall tender
False victory for her to hold

Blinded by the victory
Consumed with her false pride
She'll fail to see the demon
My black soul hides inside

I weary of her conviction to
The beloved she holds so dear
I display an understanding
But selfishly don't care

I'll continue with my swank
Disregard her taut insistence
Like many women reaped before
I'll conquer her resistance

I simply can't believe
How she can be so brash
Snubbing my next ploy
To disrupt my planned advance

An invitation now I'll offer
To knock upon my door
I will eat this vixen's heart
This has always worked before

Expectation now rings true
I knew that she would call
Satisfaction again is mine
Her soul will take the fall

The voice I know is hers
But the retort, it is all wrong
I persist for explanation
The line's gone dead, she's gone

How can I be discharged?
These reasons are not clear
I had her in my grasp
This woman has no fear

I did not respect her second
Her sword cuts deep at me
The strength of two now present
I'm cut off below the knees

The specter of her partner
Unseen but felt so near
Soon our paths will also cross
He too will have no fear

Until another is offered
I'll heal the pride that stings
I will feed upon another
She's waiting in the wings

I care not if love exists
I must possess the soul
I scoff the one who preaches
The enlightened one in gold

So I hunt the traits again
The four that feed my pride
Love is not on the list
But that is *why men lie!*

© 2003 by Michael Rizzo

Chapter Fifteen

KOVACK

Ever since that day the portal opened, he's called me VW. I've called him Merchant.

It was a barren early-winter day, just after the solstice. We had been experiencing uncharacteristically bitter weather for the onset of the season. The furnace seemed to run all night. Much earlier, as I lay in flannel with my bare back against Michael, I could hear the snow crunch and compress under the tires of sporadically passing cars. As I pushed the covers aside to face my day, the nestling warmth of our bed seemed such a contrast to the harsh reality beyond the window.

The skies were monotone gray, much like the dull chain-link fence in the yard. I greeted Kovack at the door, trying to appear unaffected by the biting cold. I stood in bare feet, shorts, and a tank top, my usual working attire. Could feel my nose hairs freeze as the moisture from my greeting crystallized before my face.

"Jesus shittin' Christ, it's cold," he muttered. "This weather will put some stiff in your shorts," he added as if the last part was completely necessary to make his point.

Kovack (I rarely called him Jack; his real name is John) may just be the most matchless man I ever crossed paths with. Vastly different from all my other patients and certainly one of my favorites. When I met Kovack, he was sixty-six. Retired from law enforcement. Retired from private investigative work. Retired from arson squad. Not retired from drinking and carrying on.

Would never retire from giving you the best opinion on any subject—his. One tough, gritty, spittin' son of a bitch.

I didn't ask for him. He was referred to my practice by his wife, Joyce. I did a massage event downtown at the county exec's office for Secretaries' Day. The support staff got fifteen-minute massages to thank them for their hard work. She was one of them.

As the story goes, she came home and told Kovack about this massage therapist who is really strong and who helped my neck and you would like her and maybe she could help your shoulder if you would stop being so stubborn and just give it a try. After much procrastination and avoiding the issue, Kovack decided to give "this broad" a go—what could it hurt? Besides, it just might prove to be entertaining.

And so it was that he showed up with his you-gotta-prove-it-to-me attitude on one shoulder and a sizeable chip on the other. He took one look at me, sizing me up in his PI kind of way, and said, "You're pretty small . . . not sure what you think you're gonna be able to do."

"Humor me," I responded pseudosarcastically as my blue eyes locked on his steel blue-gray ones. During that frozen moment, I acknowledged a silent conversation that passed between us though I was unsure of what, exactly, was exchanged.

I reviewed his health history. *This man should have been dead three times over by now,* I thought to myself. Routine drinker. Cigar smoker. High stress level. Coronary artery bypass surgery, twice. Gallbladder surgery. Numerous other small issues that would collectively make even the most tolerant person miserable.

While I gave direction and inquired for clarification on health issues, he listened with one ear while looking around the unfamiliar environment. I could tell by his facial expression that he was wondering just how the heck he got himself into this mess and how the hell he was going to get himself out.

Treatment for his type of shoulder injury requires much deep muscle work with heavy, sustained pressure. I attempted to prepare him by letting him know that the work might be uncomfortable and to let me know if the pressure was too much for him or if he wanted me to back off.

"Don't count on it," he snorted a laugh.

In short order, he was groaning and wincing and armoring his muscles. I gradually increased the pressure as I worked my knuckles deeper into his sub-shoulder blade area.

"OK?" I asked, fully understanding that he was not.

"Yeah," he squeezed out.

I smiled knowingly to myself. Now it would be very hard for him to ask me to back off.

"Don't be a hero," I added gently.

"Uncle!" he gasped.

After this mock battle, we settled into a nice temperate routine: we quickly achieved a tacit understanding of the rules of engagement.

Turns out, about three days later, he phoned. "Jezuss Christ! You kicked my ass—but the shoulder feels great, babe." He calls everyone he likes "babe."

"I can finally get my arm above my head. Outstanding!" His enthusiasm was almost more than I could bear. "Book me!"

And so it went. One hour once a month, with a brief hiatus when he traveled to Florida from January through April. He became for me a great study in paradox as well as a tight friend. The environment in which we worked lent well to security and trust, and we both began to open up and commiserate over our darkest deeds, most profound thoughts, and largely brilliant observations. Hard and stoic exterior, tough, prickly, tenacious. Goddamning all over the place. Yet his coarse exterior protected and housed a most sensitive, thoughtful, injured, feeling person. Both sides quickly endeared themselves to me.

We talked through the entire massage, every massage. Each story he told presented a parallel invitation to evoke my surprisingly similar admission, and vice versa. At times, my "confessions" gave birth to one of his very much like my own. Dangerous waters to wade in, one might say. A breach of ethics, might say another, inappropriate for a practitioner-patient relationship. However, it was what it was, and this was the stuff of our relationship. Tacit, genderless acceptance scaffolded by an unforgiving, nothing-held-back, cut-you-no-slack manner. The room was always loaded with raucous, irreverent humor—laughing at ourselves like no one else could or would even dare.

On this chilling morning of our fifth year together, I was to face an unforeseen event that would forever fortify me. Later that afternoon, I would share it with Kovack. His response still makes my skin prickle to this day.

The girls were off from school, so we decided to make a fire and hole up in the living room for the morning. After securing the necessary provisions from our kitchen (hot chocolate and graham crackers), we settled in near the hearth to forget the view outside the windows for a few hours.

Heather on the floor, Shannon on the couch. I positioned myself on the rocking chair facing the hearth so that my bare feet could receive the warmth first. I did not have anything I was particularly interested in reading and wasn't feeling up to writing just then. I contented myself with staring into the ever-changing glow. Celtic music played softly from the corner.

My children were unusually quiet; a fire, I found when they were very young, had this effect on them. Each of us was still, warmed by thoughts the flames brought forth.

As I became entranced in the glow, an incredibly somber feeling overtook me. I continued to watch the fire-play and ember-surges as I came to further define the feeling. I was experiencing a profound sense of foreboding, with a surprisingly calm acceptance of it. My mouth became dry, and I detected a slight metallic taste. My breathing deepened and grew purposeful. I knew that something I could not stop was due to happen. Something made of duty and necessity in which I would have to participate, though it was not clear what.

A sharp wind kicked up from my flank, fueling combustion as it blew past my shoulders, which felt surprisingly stiff and exposed. The fresh supply of cold air forced the flames higher, and I could feel the front of my brow begin to sear. With a watchful eye on the fire, I raised my hand to shield my forehead. How peculiar that my fingers were so rough! I had, I thought, taken the time in the morning to be certain that my hands were smooth and sandpaper-spot free. Had I forgotten to do it?

I pulled my hand down to check out the inconsistency. What I saw stunned me so much that the tidal volume filling my lungs had to be consciously and forcefully released. I found myself staring down at a great hand, one easily twice the size of my own. Instinctively, I shot a glance to what was another identical hand resting on my leg, which was draped in tattered open-weave cloth. Cracked hornlike nails packed with dirt. Knurly, knobby knuckles. Old scars, new cuts. Something that looked like dried blood, though in the firelight, I could not be certain. I turned these hands over, finding much of the same. Attempting to force open the arthritic mass was quite painful. My palms were raw, the bones and deep muscles were throbbing like a measured kettledrum beat.

Slowly, I looked aside in the darkness to meet the eyes of another. A motionless man sitting adjacent to me, his dirty face lit by the orange glow. A large man. Burly. Long light brown hair, tangled hairs on his upper lip. An even longer beard, some of it stuck in clumps with an oily-looking substance. Cuts. Scrapes. Scars, bruises, blood. Tired. Bare chested in spite of the light snow on his sacklike boots.

I could see from his gaze that I was much like him. We locked eyes but said nothing. The man I did not recognize, but his eyes I easily did. I knew them in an instant—I have stared into these eyes a thousand times, with every range of emotion.

Hesitantly, I broke the silent conversation to look about elsewhere. He watched me as I scanned the encampment. A black sky lit by many small fires, men huddled for warmth. Shields. Armor. Mumbling. Swords on sharpening stones. Flesh of some beast charring over a rudimentary spit. Sweat and metal.

I found myself scratching my chest through my reddish blond beard. Yes. My amulet on its leather strap had also survived the day. The heart of the flames caught my watch again. I paused, then rested my bare forearms on my knees. I leaned in.

Out beyond the fire, a small panic-stricken voice inconsistent with the harsh setting called to me. A child? More than one? All at once, I felt light and agile. I raised my head from the flames and found myself looking directly into the panicked expressions of my girls, each of their faces about six inches from my own.

With a terrified look on her face, Shannon was screaming my name. Heather was visibly shaken; she told me that she had been calling me for a long time. She wanted to know why I wouldn't answer. I drew my hands to their cheeks. I did not know what to tell them. I hugged them and calmed them and told them that I was all right.

For the remainder of the morning, I was intense and focused, going over and over again what I had seen, where I had been. My logical brain struggled to explain it away. My intuitive self immediately recognized it for what it was. By the end of lunch, every cell in my body convinced me of what had happened.

Kovack leaned back to lock his car—Honda Accord: for the money, best goddamned car you can park your dupa in—and continued, "Can't wait to get the hell out of this horseshit, babe. Freakin' cold 'as got my nuts in the wringer."

"Get your whining carcass inside," I said with a smile, always glad to see him. "Since I have no choice about listening to you bitch, at least let me do it where it's warm."

During our usual exchange of pleasantries and unpleasantries, he seemed to study me. He was participating in the conversation sure enough, but clearly, the more analytical cross-referencing section of his dogin (his word for brain) was attempting to solve the mystery of what my expression was saying.

He interrupted me, "You're holding out on me, babe. What's going on?" I paused. He prodded, "What happened to you?"

Couldn't hide it. Didn't really want to. "Get yourself on the table, Kovack, then I'll talk," I said, making a deal with him. As I turned to leave the room, I couldn't help but imagine him interrogating a suspect. "Yell 'ready' when you are."

"You da boss!" I heard as the door closed behind me, muffling the bellow.

I began to work the bulky muscles of his thick back. "Kovack," I started softly, "the most amazing thing happened this morning."

"Michael thinks you guys should get married?" He laughed heartily at his own joke, one I would have normally found quite funny.

"No, more amazing than that," I said plainly.

Hearing in my voice that it was not a comic moment, he apologetically asked me to go on.

As I labored, I relayed the events that occurred at my hearth—that in a past lifetime, I was a Norseman of some type. I had fought all that day until the weary sun set. It was a difficult, costly battle. I had to do the same again at daybreak. My friend or my brother or my fighting partner had been in the clash alongside me. We fought well together.

"He had Michael's eyes, Jack." I paused at hearing myself say it. "It *was* Michael." I continued to work, my heart racing as I recounted the rest of the adventure.

"I was there. The sting of the cold on my unclothed skin, the pain in my hands, the ache of my body. The stench, the grime of the battle, the exhaustion. The knowing what the sunrise would bring."

I told him how my girls brought me back. How I came to understand in the hours preceding his appointment that I had a brief albeit significant exposure to what was, what *had to have been*, a past life.

"I was a Viking warrior, Jack," I continued slowly along with the rhythmic motions of my body against his. "It's not something I ever thought about or dreamed of or conjured or contrived or wished upon myself. About two hours ago, I was allowed to witness that I was an ancient fighting man trying to see through to the end of a great battle," I concluded with much conviction.

My fountain trickled supportively in the corner. The wind pressed the glass of the windows. Stirring bagpipes settled serene in my ears. My breathing was strong and measured. We both listened to the silence beneath the ambient sounds.

For a long while, Kovack said nothing. Instead, his body began to speak for him. I felt his muscles tense under my hands. I had the sense his body was wrestling with his mind and felt an undercurrent of agitation just below his skin. He took a long breath then held it. Finally, he exhaled deeply, almost as if to allow my palms to sink directly into his trunk. His entire body softened under my touch.

"I was a merchant," he started quietly but with much certainty. "I owned a shop, in a whaling town—Boston, 1700s. I had dried goods, provisions. Bric-a-brac, sundries, seasonal stuff. It was small, but neat, clean. Organized . . . You get the picture." It was the first time I ever heard him speak so softly. "My office had a window, like the stern of a wooden sailing vessel—you know, the captain's galley. My desk was there, facing the window, looking out over the harbor. Just like I was in a ship. I would walk down a flight of a few stairs to get to my store."

He continued with rising adamant inflection, yet his body remained soft. "I had an Irish-sounding name. I was wealthy. I'm not sure where I initially got the money from. I was rich, but I was lonely. After I would lock up for the night, I would walk the cobbled streets . . . like I was searching. I have known this since I was a boy."

A few moments passed. "I have never told anyone of this, not even my wife. It feels so good to finally hear myself say it. It's not the kind of thing a bastard like me goes around talking about. Hearing you speak of your past life tells me mine is real."

I thought he had finished, but he added, almost as if what was to follow was more unbelievable than what preceded it. "You would often come into my shop. I've known it was you from the first time we met . . . when I saw your eyes."

"Holy shit," I remarked.

The hour was going fast, and our communication gates were open wide. My mind was working at a feverish speed; I had to force my body to keep a slowed, metronome pace as I worked. I shared with him my sense that lives cycle together. Spirits intertwine and souls cross again and again. We both agreed our relationship was evidence of this.

Too quickly, our time passed. I had worked hard, Kovack's old body was palliated, and we were both enlightened and satisfied by our exchange. Before I left the room, as always when completing a massage, I performed gasho; it felt unexpectedly authentic and sacred.

I washed from my shoulders to my hands with foamy white soap. Kovack dressed. I reentered my room with a glass of water and a smile. I looked at him. He looked at me.

"Well, I'll be damned!" he exclaimed. "A Viking warrior! Now that explains a hell of a lot!" He added, "You kicked my ass and took names, VW."

"Yes, merchant," I replied with a fulfilled smile. "Indeed . . . I did."

Now I'm not saying the "I" that is me now was a Viking warrior. Or the Jack as he is today was the merchant of yesteryear. What I *am* saying is that energy recycles. Spiritual, soul energy cannot be created or destroyed. When you are born, the stuff that makes us the persons we are is drawn from a collective crucible of energy; when we die, it returns to the cauldron only to be stirred and withdrawn again.

I am not alone in believing that we have all been men, women, children, warriors, and merchants. Light people, dark people, slaves, and aristocracy. The highest organizational power retains some of that memory, and it manifests itself again in a flashback, a past-life vision, or perhaps just a sense that we were *there*.

More evolved souls have used each life to grow and change. More enlightened people have spent many lives back and forth between male and female form, young and old. Have felt the empathy of being in yet another unique situation. These experiences imprint on the part of you that is timeless and manifest in different beings over the time continuum.

Each act of courage, every obstacle overcome, each lesson learned, every temptation thwarted builds our soul up so that we may better handle the next discernable life our spirit takes. It's so important to lighten our karmic debt. Free ourselves from the shackles that aberrant deeds of this lifetime clasp upon our wrists so that we may progress further in the next. Understand and see the importance of our connection to the past and our effect on the future. Act as if this life we have now is a day in the subsistence of the universe.

Since that day, I have shared my experience with many others, and I am no longer surprised to find that it is very common. Many, if not all, of us have these senses or experiences, yet we hesitate to announce them. To discuss them. To draw from them. Perhaps because it seems too bizarre, too existential, too unsafe to talk about. Or the concept is too easily subject to ridicule.

Do you have a particular draw toward a period in time? Do you feel so clearly that you were present in another place at another time but in a different body? Do you have an unexplained penchant for period wear or certain collectables? Perhaps a recurring "daydream" of a simple event much too far in the past for you to have such intimate knowledge of?

Of course you have. Do not let anyone tell you that we are born, we live, we die, and that's it. Do not allow anyone to dismiss what every cell in your body knows—that we have been here before, we are here for a short time, and we will be back again.

Epilogue

MARY BETH

Mary Beth loved her three younger brothers. She felt purpose and direction when they were in her charge, was proud that she could read them stories and make them peanut-butter-and-jelly sandwiches with the crust cut off. It was important that she knew how to gauge their body language, significant that they coexisted on a connected, unspoken level. It *mattered* that the bleached white cloth diapers from the line in the yard were folded into exactly perfect rectangles for her baby brother. It was providence that she had one hand for each of her other brothers to hold.

Mary Beth felt indispensable when they would run to her crying or hurt. She put whatever else aside, sat next to them on the step, or heaved them onto her lap. She gladly wiped their noses and dabbed their tears. To effectively lull a sobbing child felt like the most vital power in the world. And she was *good* at this!

On late Sunday night drives back from Grandma's house in Buffalo, she would sit with them in the backseat of the Oldsmobile. It was late, and they were all very tired. Brian would sleep on the floor with his head on the hump, and Mary Beth would put her bare legs oh-so-gently on the outside of him so that he was cradled behind her calves. Mark would often lie to her left, his thick sandy-blonde hair on her exposed shoulder. Paul was usually to her right, his little head on her tiny lap. She would hold the side of Mark's face with one hand while smoothing Paul's fine flaxen hair with the other. She could smell play and sleep on them. She loved them; they loved her. They called her Mare.

Mare didn't dare fall asleep. She needed to stay awake and watch over them. Not that anything could possibly happen to them in the backseat of the family car, but that was hardly the point. She would lean her head back on the worn maroon leather seat and look into the darkness passing outside the half-open window, forcing herself to stay awake.

Ever since that first-grade field trip to the planetarium, she would search the blackness for Orion. She would find his belt and envision where the sword was sheathed then move her eyes to locate the stars that marked his broad muscular shoulders, supporting brawny arms ending in thick hands. Finding the glow that marked his forehead was easy. For a time, she would gaze upon his ebony face before locating the lights that sketched his massive thighs and thick calves. Once she had a fix on his form, she would watch impermanent landmarks pass while he stoically watched from above in his battle-ready pose. Occasionally, that spotlight panning the sky from she-knew-not-where would momentarily obscure him, but he would always reappear.

At times, Mary Beth would turn her attention to her parents in the front seat. Her father always drove. She could just make out the neckline of his threadbare cotton undershirt and his pale skin coming from it. He would stare straight on with unblinking eyelashless lids. Without the use of his fingers, he'd take a drag on the Pall Mall stuck in the right side of his tight thin lips. Sucking on the cigarette would cause the glowing end to brighten in the dark, and she could see the ember creep toward his face—he smoked them down so far that she was certain he would burn his lip someday. He would pause for a moment then, without moving his head or taking the butt from his mouth, empty his lungs toward the open window. *So unlike Orion*, she thought.

On the other side of the front seat sat her mother, usually asleep by this time. She rested her scarf-tied head on the doorframe and, though her eyes were closed, still wore her dark-rimmed cat glasses with teeny rhinestones in the corners. She always looked busy, always looked tired. She *did* think of clever ways to remember state capitals and made cookies for school lunches. Grandma was *her* mother. They seemed so different.

Mary Beth would glance from one parent to the next and then back again. She didn't understand her parents; they did not know their offspring. She wondered just who they were and why they liked each other. She knew that she was somehow a product of their marriage but was not yet old enough to understand the mechanics. Or the implications.

Mare looked down again upon her brothers. They were sweet, made her laugh. Though they never said it, she knew that during *that* era, they looked up to her. But they all grew up, grew apart. Grew away. All that really mattered to her was gone.

Mary Beth was blessed—and simultaneously cursed—with an acutely present mind. One that saw things for what they were long before she had the awareness to name them aptly. Way before she understood the implications of what transpired before her young watch. Far prior to developing a vantage point for appropriate reflection. She retained many things that others told her she could not possibly have remembered. *And* was informed that she was wrong about her interpretations anyway.

Long after she was finally broken of the push to wonder out loud about these observations, she continued to inquire vigilantly with her scanning blue yes. The sensible world usually implied one thing. However, her body was of the ages and most often adamantly disagreed. In order to preserve the integrity and secure the survival of the perceptions, her body sequestered them. Seized what every cell knew and infused the truths into her tissues until such time that they would be called up.

On the surface of this young child was no discernable evidence of all that her body submerged, but a heavy current of sorrow churned far below where no light could reach. Only minuscule glimpses of the unrest manifested themselves and were missed or ignored. Her developing habit of harsh criticism of others reflected her unhappiness, and she began to lie. Her shell moved through most days in an automatic manner, and she looked to the expectations put on her with dread and resentment. At times, she was pushed through her days; often, she was pulled. Little seemed to be of her own volition.

This went on for a lifetime. When one does not care, and one does not hope, it is easy to engage in self-destructive behavior. It is simple to do what feels necessary to survive. Disconnectedness begets isolation: she was adrift and dehydrated with no sign of a horizon.

Many years into her adulthood, Mary Beth found herself raising her head from the ancient undertow of unhappiness, relentlessly pulling toward the depths. Perhaps a professional, she considered, could provide some direction and sustenance. She was given the name of a psychotherapist who came highly recommended by someone who once mattered and made the call.

Mary Beth needed labels. The inquisitive mind she entertained wanted to know exactly what was what and why it was that way. Many months of stalled therapy passed. On a whim, she asked the psychotherapist exactly what her diagnosis was; she wanted to know the actual clinical term for the cause of the despair and discontent in her life.

The woman hesitated. Mary Beth pushed and told her that it was important that she know the name of this entity. The psychotherapist exhaled quietly then told her client that the issue was fear of intimacy. That she was presently unable to allow herself to trust another person. That in her professional opinion, much of the reason why her client struggled was due to the inability to enter into true confidence in relationships and unwillingness to put herself in the risky position of trusting another human being. Mary Beth was hoping for something a bit more scientific and clinical sounding—this was rudimentary. So simple. But oh-so-difficult to overcome.

Sadly, she saw that the psychotherapist was right. Prior to the series of events that set her free, she held few genuine relationships. She had many contacts, casual acquaintances, and peripheral associations. Most of the dealings were in a one-way direction: Mary Beth made a common assumption that people were present for her benefit. With most cases, she only allowed people to see of herself what she chose to reveal. Most individuals were viewed as a one-way valve to the next opportunity. Aside from those few notable exceptions, she used people up.

The burden of knowing made her pain worse. In the following dark moments of clarity, it became apparent how this reality affected her days. Her years. Her life. Mary Beth grasped the gravity of the situation quickly. Her body felt terrible. Like she had been hit by a tidal wave and thrown broken and battered onto a gravelly beachhead. She knew that to reverse the trend of her present chosen existence would take catastrophic upheaval and a cataclysmic shift. Her entire body screamed for her to do something. She felt helpless; the situation seemed hopeless. She went home and held her babies, seemingly the only pure relationships she could claim. After she put them to sleep, she had a sizeable glass of wine. Maybe another. Where to start? She cried.

Early the next morning, she sat at the small kitchen table made from the frame of an old-fashioned sewing machine. She reached over her mug of black coffee to pick up the paper. Read the comics first, followed by Dear Abby, then casually returned to the front of the section. It was then that a small article—on what would ultimately play a hand in her liberation—caught her eye. It was not a half-page spread, just a little blip in the bottom corner about the recent interest in massage therapy as a developing profession.

All in an instant, her entire body straightened and surged a resounding, "Yes!" Mary Beth put the paper down and filled her lungs, felt her heart pound deep and determined. She didn't understand how but felt the answer *had* come. In a breath short of disbelief, she thought back to yesterday. For not even a day prior, she sat in stringent evaluation of all that comprised her unfulfilled life.

Deliberation came to her job. She thought hard about why she liked being a dental hygienist: she was comfortable touching people and helping them, enjoyed the medical acclimation and health emphasis of the profession. Easily called up the didactic knowledge of the body necessary to do the job well, often felt significant providing direction and assisting in another's move toward well-being. It sadly occurred to her that teeth had nothing to do with any of that. Yesterday, she sighed despondently. Not one thing in her life seemed to be *exactly* right.

But that was yesterday. She took another sip of coffee. Today was a fresh day. Her pulse quickened as she felt a sense of hope well inside her, the likes of which had not been felt in a very long time. The events of the last twenty-four hours *meant* something. The events that she ignored for *years* meant something. It became apparent when she pushed against a process that she was searching all the time and never had what she needed; swiftly remembered that when she gave in to the benevolent Universe she knew existed, things were smoother and what she required materialized. As a child, she knew this; as a very young person, she lived it. Gradually, the natural channel was blocked and silenced by those distractions that diverted her attention. Some seemingly innocuous things—and many that were not—decreased her acuity and sensitivity to the subtle forces that previously *did* and still *could* govern her existence. She left it behind, all but forgot. But her body remembered, and her body reminded—the always-present forces of the Universe *did not* abandon her. Suddenly, she knew she would follow the sign.

There is a wonderful world of happenstance, intuition, and incidence waiting just below the surface of everyday life: the Universe orchestrates our world so that we may attain happiness and fulfillment. Through our hours and days and years, the force that created us continues to offer nurturance and guidance. Woven in and out through our life, the Universe places opportunity and occasion in close proximity to us so that we may negotiate a shift when needed. The markers are ever present and in attendance without exception. Sometimes, they come to us through another person; at times, by way of something else. But they are always and forever placed before us. Even on our dying day, we still have one last chance to get it right.

At the moment of going under, she was thrown a line. The reconnection to her true self set her on the journey of healing. On looking back, it is still absolutely amazing to Mare that once she made the decision to start out on that uncertain crossing, the Universe placed everything necessary before her when it was needed. The unique circumstances that defined massage therapy established a reparenting of sorts, a template for true responsibility and intimacy from which to reconstruct. Everything that was at hand in the beginning was still *there*. She had just gotten so far away from it. Mare's soul was an abandoned child. Her hands are the surrogate mother who saved it.

For her, redemption could not happen in a vacuum. Enlightenment would not occur at some remote mountaintop retreat. Deliverance was not to arise from isolation. Mare had to find herself in the intimate presence of others. Genuine reconnection with people was critical in order to get past herself. Equally as crucial was relearning to rely on and trust the infallible compass that was her body. Deferring to the Universe, paramount.

Mare took one last sip and peered into the bottom of the bare mug. She cradled the thick porcelain in both hands while tilting it back to look at it. In spite of being empty, it was still warm. She had it for a very long time. It was her absolute favorite mug, the only one she would drink her morning coffee from. With an enlightened smile, it occurred to her that her coffee mug summarized what she admired and respected most in this world and represented what really mattered.

It was waiting for her, way back on a secluded shelf at the flea market. Found while not sought. Simple in form, an easy concave shape. Very solid, sturdy grade. Strong with a dependable grip. It was old, utilized and washed thousands of times, held by many other hands. Bone colored with unpretentious light blue female and male figures encircling the outside, their arms upraised and joined in joy where their hands would be.

Acknowledgements

I would like to thank the following people who participated in focus groups for this book, graciously volunteering their time, effort, and energy. All provided a refreshing external perspective for me in preparation for fine-tuning my manuscript. Without a doubt, each will see their subtle hand in my work.

Group 1

Kirk Chilas
Laura Kriegel
Glynis Kristal-Ragsdale
Heather Swenson
Shannon Swenson

Group 2

Mary Bausch
Rick Bausch
Susan Boudreaux
Michael Rizzo

Group 3

Lin Owen-Dean
Todd DeKramer, LMT
Judy Fletcher, LMT

Group 4

Ellen Carr*
Larry Weld
Paul Jordan

Group 5

Katherine Johnson-Milton
Angela Pignata
Guy Rossi
Judy Rossi

* Special thanks to Ellen for her review of the entire manuscript and the critical feedback she provided. Her insight and objectivity filled in where mine was missing.

More special thanks to Gerry Egeling for the same.

Lesley Brooks-Bianchi gave me a wonderful manicure in preparation for the cover photo. My hands can tell that her hands love what they do.

Sara Lovell applied makeup for my cover portrait so skillfully that it did not look like I was wearing much at all.

Teri Fiske, owner of Pumpkin Patch Photos, worked skillfully with my vision for a cover photo.

Most importantly, thank you, Michael. You provided a complete range of support during the entire process. You even knew when to do nothing. This book would not be what it is without your choice to be present in my life. I love you.